Hoermann

D1788709

125 Ways To Be A Better Listener™

A Program for Listening Success

Nan Stutzman Graser

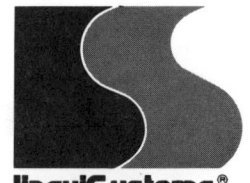

LinguiSystems®
LinguiSystems, Inc.
3100 4th Avenue
East Moline, IL 61244

Skill Area: Listening
Grade Level: 7th grade thru Adult

Printed in the U.S.A.

1-800-PRO IDEA
1-800-776-4332

ISBN 1-55999-232-8

About the Author

Nan Stutzman Graser, M.A., CCC, is a speech-language pathologist in the public school system and in private practice. Since graduating from Northwestern University, she has provided services to regular and special education children and adults in suburban Chicago for six years. Nan's professional interests include listening strategies, voice, and phonological articulation intervention.

August 1992

Dedication

To my father, Dr. Robert L. Stutzman, one of the most skillful listeners I have ever known.

Acknowledgments

Terry, Tracie, Bill, and friends at KH for your valuable suggestions, contributions, and encouragement.

"For you and your students —
The best language, learning, and thinking materials.
LinguiSystems' promise to you."

We welcome your comments on *125 Ways to Be a Better Listener* and other LinguiSystems products. Please send your comments to Carolyn Blagden, Editor in Chief.

Editors: Mary McIntyre, Kamala Simonton
Designer: Beth Ducey
Illustrator: Tami Schmidt
Desktop Publisher: Jennifer Kay

Table of Contents

Introduction

Students with poor and passive listening behaviors are plentiful. So, too, are opportunities for listening during a student's typical day. In school, the amount of time students spend listening greatly outweighs the amount of time they spend communicating in other ways, such as speaking, reading, and writing. In fact, as students move from elementary to junior and senior high school, the requirements for listening increase significantly.

125 Ways to Be a Better Listener addresses the needs of students who have weak auditory attention, memory, and comprehension skills. This book offers your students 125 strategies for improving their active listening. We've provided a list of all 125 strategies beginning on page 7. You might want to make copies of the list to discuss with your students before, during or after completing each unit. Or, make a transparency of the list to use on an overhead projector. However you use the list, your students are given the opportunity to practice these strategies in a variety of communication settings, including home, school, and work. Your students need to realize that effective, sincere listening is important to their academic, social, and vocational success.

We suggest you teach the strategies in the order in which they're given. This way, your students will learn simple strategies — like listening for information and paying attention — before they learn more complex strategies — like listening for the main idea and giving nonverbal feedback. Here's a short summary of the five units.

- *What Is Listening?* explains the process of listening and introduces four types of listening.

- *Giving Direction to Your Listening* describes the four types of listening in more detail.

- *Getting Ready to Listen* gives your students hints for improving their listening attitudes and for dealing with the distractions that so often inhibit good listening.

- *Being an Active Listener* explains how your students can visualize, repeat messages, and listen for what's important.

- *Responding to the Message* gives your students tips for giving feedback and asking clarifying questions.

Each unit begins with an introduction called *Teacher Tips*. These tips tell you what the unit is about and includes goals for the unit. Following the *Teacher Tips* are suggestions for discussing the handouts with your students, helping them complete the activity sheets, and providing your students with further practice of the strategies. Finally, on the last page of each unit, you'll find additional activities your whole class will enjoy.

These suggestions, however, are simply guidelines. Since you know your students best, feel free to modify the handouts and activities in ways that will be most beneficial to your students. And don't forget to model effective listening behaviors yourself! If you want your students to be good listeners, you have to be a good listener.

As your students become familiar with a wide variety of listening strategies, they'll demonstrate active listening behaviors. Your students' auditory skills can improve once they're given the "how to" techniques to build better listening. *125 Ways to Be a Better Listener* gives your students the tools they need to be capable, active listeners.

Nan Stutzman Graser

125 Ways to Be a Better Listener

Unit 2: Giving Direction to Your Listening

5 Ways to Listen for Enjoyment	page 34

1. Think about the things you like to listen to.

2. Listen for enjoyment by yourself.

3. Listen for enjoyment with other people.

4. Let your friends choose music or TV shows they like.

5. Remember, the time you spend in appreciative listening isn't time wasted.

9 Ways to Listen with Understanding	pages 36 to 38

6. Listen without adding your own ideas about what your friend is feeling.

7. Say your friend's name during the conversation.

8. Keep your friend's point of view in mind.

9. Respond to your friend with words and actions.

10. Encourage your friend to keep talking.

11. Encourage your friend to solve her own problems.

12. Even if your friend has done something or said something you disapprove of, try not to show your disapproval.

13. Let your friend know that his feelings are acceptable.

14. Understand that you won't always know what to say or how to help your friends solve their problems.

6 Ways to Listen for Information   pages 41 and 42

15   Know when to use comprehensive listening.

16   Concentrate on the situation.

17   Use your five senses.

18   Listen for important information.

19   Ask questions.

20   Repeat the message.

7 Ways to Evaluate a Message   pages 44 and 45

21   Think about the information you've heard.

22   Decide if you can trust the information.

23   Learn to pick out opinions that sound like facts.

24   Listen to the whole message before you make your decision.

25   If you're not sure you can judge a message, ask questions.

26   Understand that different people respond differently to the same message.

27   Decide to accept or reject the speaker's message.

4 Ways to Evaluate Commercials   pages 46 and 47

28   Beware of tricky advertising.

29   Listen for emotional appeals.

30   Be aware of sweeping cause statements.

31   Decide if you can trust the speaker.

Unit 3: Getting Ready to Listen

5 Tips About Your Listening Attention Level (LAL)   pages 60 and 61

32   Imagine a scale from 0 to 5. 0 stands for low attention needed for listening, and 5 stands for high attention needed for listening.

33   Be aware of your current LAL.

34   Recognize that different LALs are needed at different times.

35   Ask questions about the listening activity you're getting ready for.

36   Decide what LAL you'll need for the new listening situation.

7 Ways to Change Your LAL   page 64

37   Decide if you need to change your LAL.

38   Raise your LAL if necessary by changing your posture.

39   Raise your LAL by taking a quick, deep breath.

40   Raise your LAL by facing the speaker.

41   Raise your LAL by moving closer to the speaker, if possible.

42   Lower your LAL by taking a slow, deep breath.

43   Lower your LAL by relaxing your posture.

8 Ways to Identify Distractions   pages 67 and 68

44   Know what a *distraction* is.

45   Ask, "What do I see or hear that's keeping me from listening?"

46   Ask, "What is it about the room that's making it hard for me to listen?"

47   Ask, "Is there anything about the way I'm feeling that's making it hard to be a good listener?"

48   Ask, "Are my emotions getting in the way of good listening?"

49   Ask, "Is there anything about the speaker that's keeping me from listening?"

50   Ask, "What is my attitude toward listening?"

51   Realize that you and the people around you might not be bothered by the same things.

4 Ways to Get Rid of Distractions   page 71

52   Identify distractions when you begin listening.

53   Ask yourself if you can get rid of the distraction.

54   Change the environment if you can.

55   Set aside the distraction.

5 Ways to Pay Attention   page 72

56   Know what you're going to be listening to.

57   Know why you're listening.

58   Identify distractions.

59   Decide what you can do about the distractions.

60   Relate the topic to your own life.

61   Have a "wait and see" attitude.

62   Think of positive outcomes of what you're about to hear.

63   Don't expect the speaker to entertain you.

64   Let your posture help your attitude.

65   Change negative self-talk to positive self-talk.

66   Check your attitude as you listen.

67   Thank the speaker for sharing his ideas.

68   Remember that good listening improves your relationships.

Unit 4: Being an Active Listener

8 Ways to Picture Messages in Your Mind   **pages 84 and 85**

69   Try to see what you hear.

70   Close your eyes.

71   Use all your senses when you make pictures in your mind.

72   Add emotions and feelings to your pictures.

73   Think of words to go with your pictures.

74   Be creative.

75   Make the action words you hear come alive.

76   Draw a picture of the new idea.

8 Ways to Remember Short Messages   **pages 92 and 93**

77   Repeat words, phrases, and short sentences to yourself.

78   Use your mind's ear to remember people's names.

79   Use your mind's ear to remember main ideas.

80   Use your mind's ear to remember short messages.

81   Write the message down as soon as possible.

82   Use your mind's ear to "think along" with the speaker.

83   Use your mind's eye and mind's ear at the same time.

84   Decide if the information you just heard makes sense.

7 Ways to Remember Long Messages

pages 96 and 97

85   Know the topic of the message.

86   See if the speaker writes what he says.

87   Use your mind's eye.

88   Use your mind's ear.

89   Don't repeat the message word for word.

90   Take notes.

91   Relate the new information to information you already know.

6 Ways to Listen for What's Important

pages 98 to 100

92   Listen for the main idea.

93   Listen to the speaker's voice.

94   Listen for the speaker to repeat herself.

95   Listen for signal words.

96   Listen for other important words.

97   Ask yourself questions.

125 Ways to Be a Better Listener

13

Unit 5: Responding to the Message

5 Ways to Give Verbal Feedback

98 Decide when you should give verbal feedback.

99 Practice giving verbal feedback.

100 Don't judge the speaker.

101 Show you're interested in the speaker's topic.

102 When the speaker is finished, share any information you have.

5 Ways to Improve Your Verbal Feedback

103 Give specific feedback.

104 When possible, give immediate feedback.

105 Give the speaker feedback when he asks for it.

106 Thank the speaker for his time and information.

107 Realize that your feedback might not be rewarded.

9 Ways to Give Nonverbal Feedback

108 Face the speaker.

109 Make eye contact.

110 Sit up straight.

111 Take notes.

112   Use facial expressions.

113   Give nonverbal feedback often.

114   Give nonverbal feedback at any time during a speaker's message.

115   Watch for nonverbal feedback that sends a negative message.

116   Be careful not to send "mixed messages."

9 Tips for Asking Questions   pages 118 and 119

117   Wait until the speaker has finished before you ask questions.

118   Write questions down as you think of them.

119   Ask specific questions.

120   Try to ask questions that are related to the topic.

121   Ask the speaker to define words you don't know.

122   Tell the speaker if you missed part of her message.

123   If you're not sure what a message means, ask the speaker to explain it again.

124   Remember, any question that helps you understand is a good question.

125   Restate what you think the speaker said.

Unit 1: What Is Listening?

Teacher Tips

3 handouts, pages 20 to 22
2 activity sheets, pages 23 to 25

Do your students know what listening is? Do they realize they can improve their listening skills? Do they know that hearing isn't the same as listening? This unit will help your students understand what listening is and introduce four types of listening to them.

First, ask your students what they think listening is. You might ask questions like, "Is listening only hearing?" or "If your ears work, does that make you a good listener?"

Give each student copies of the handouts. Talk about the different aspects of listening, such as hearing, understanding, and remembering. Then, spend some time discussing why it's important to be a good listener and the responsibilities your students have as listeners.

Next, have your students complete the activity sheets. When your students are finished, talk about their reasons for listening, why they want to improve their listening, and why listening is important.

Handout: The Process of Listening

This handout will help your students understand the process of listening. First, discuss the chart and the average amount of time people spend on each type of communication. Next, talk about the six steps that make up the process of listening. Finally, help your students think of examples for each step in the listening process.

Handout: Listening Myths

The second handout lists five common misconceptions your students might have about listening. Have your students take turns reading the myths. Then, discuss why each idea is incorrect. Stress that good listening is the *listener's* responsibility.

Handout: Types of Listening

Brainstorm different situations that require listening. Write your students' responses on the chalkboard. Talk about the different listening techniques your students would use in each situation. Then, give each student a copy of the handout and discuss the four types of listening. Next, have your students decide what type of listening matches the situations they brainstormed. Explain to your students that they'll study appreciative, empathic, comprehensive, and evaluative listening in more detail in Unit 2.

Activity Sheet: Why Do You Listen?

The first activity sheet asks your students to consider the reasons they listen in different situations and settings. Use your students' responses to begin a class discussion. Talk about how different situations and settings require different types of listening.

Why Do You Listen?   Name _____

List some reasons you should listen in each situation below. Then, give an example of a time you listened in each situation and how your good listening skills helped you.

1. at school   *Answers will vary.* _____
   _____
   _____

2. at home _____
   _____
   _____

3. on the job _____
   _____
   _____

4. at a play or concert _____
   _____
   _____

5. taking a phone message for someone _____
   _____
   _____

6. at a friend's house _____
   _____
   _____

Unit 1
Activity Sheet   23   125 Ways to Be a Better Listener
                                                Copyright © 1992 LinguiSystems, Inc.

Activity Sheet: Listen Up!

This activity sheet gives your students some information about listening in and out of school. Read the first two paragraphs to your students. Then, have your students complete the activity sheet. When they're finished, discuss why listening is important in each situation and the positive effects good listening might have. Encourage your students to give personal examples related to each situation.

Listen Up!   Name _____

Almost 50% of your communication time is spent listening. If you're a good listener, you won't miss directions or assignments. You won't have to ask people to repeat themselves.

Why would good listening be important in the following situations? Give at least two reasons for each item.

1. It's your first week at a new job. Your supervisor is training you to use a computerized cash register. *to make correct change, to use the cash register correctly, to prove you're a good worker*

2. Your aunt calls to talk to your stepdad, who's not home. Your aunt decides to leave a message. *to give your stepdad the correct message, to show you're responsible*

3. Your teacher announces which chapters and vocabulary words will be on the semester test. *to study the correct information, to use your study time wisely, to do well on the test*

4. Your best friend is upset about a fight he had with his girlfriend last night. *to show your friend you care, to help your friend out, to help your friend feel better*

5. You're in charge of the props for your school theater production. The director has the cast run through Act I. *to be sure the actors have the props they need, to help the production run smoothly*

Unit 1
Activity Sheet   24   125 Ways to Be a Better Listener
                                                        Copyright © 1992 LinguiSystems, Inc.

Listen Up!   Name _____

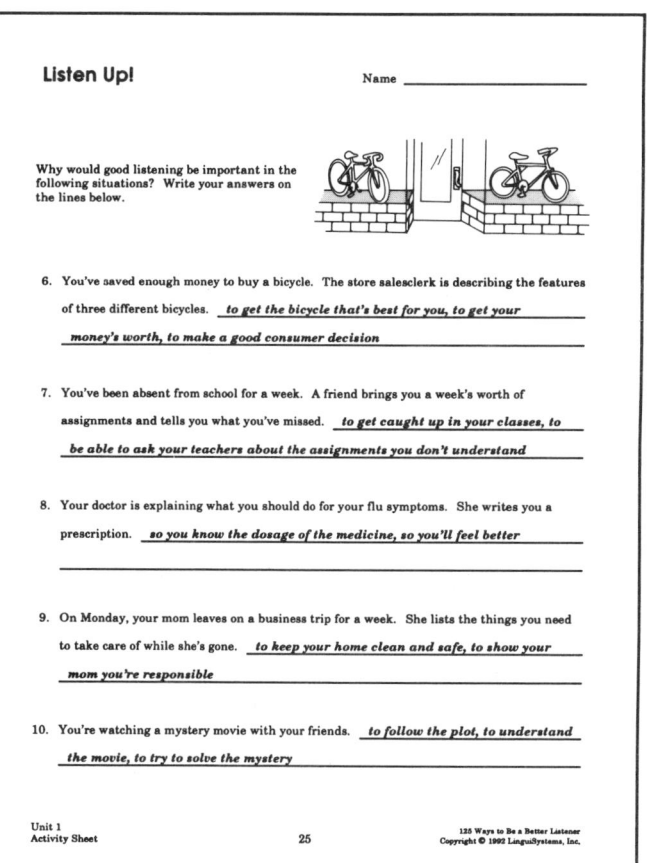

Why would good listening be important in the following situations? Write your answers on the lines below.

6. You've saved enough money to buy a bicycle. The store salesclerk is describing the features of three different bicycles. *to get the bicycle that's best for you, to get your money's worth, to make a good consumer decision*

7. You've been absent from school for a week. A friend brings you a week's worth of assignments and tells you what you've missed. *to get caught up in your classes, to be able to ask your teachers about the assignments you don't understand*

8. Your doctor is explaining what you should do for your flu symptoms. She writes you a prescription. *so you know the dosage of the medicine, so you'll feel better*

9. On Monday, your mom leaves on a business trip for a week. She lists the things you need to take care of while she's gone. *to keep your home clean and safe, to show your mom you're responsible*

10. You're watching a mystery movie with your friends. *to follow the plot, to understand the movie, to try to solve the mystery*

Unit 1
Activity Sheet   25   125 Ways to Be a Better Listener
                                                        Copyright © 1992 LinguiSystems, Inc.

The Process of Listening

Did you know that listening is a form of communication? As a matter of fact, people spend most of their communication time listening.

Since you spend so much time listening, it's a good idea to understand what listening is all about.

Listening is a process. Each step in the process is a little more difficult than the step before it.

Good listeners understand the process of listening. The six steps of listening are listed below.

Activity	Percent of Daily Communication
writing	11%
reading	15%
speaking	32%
listening	42%

Source: Richard A. Hunsaker, *Understanding and Developing the Skills of Oral Communication: Speaking and Listening*, (Englewood, CO: Morton Publishing Company, 1982).

1. **Hearing**

Hearing is the first step in listening. You hear when your ears *pick up sounds*.

2. **Paying attention**

When you *concentrate* on a sound or a speaker's message, you're paying attention.

3. **Organizing**

After you hear new information, you need to organize it. You put new information with old information that's already in your brain. In other words, you *sort new information into old categories*.

4. **Understanding**

After you sort the new information, you can begin *to make sense of it*.

5. **Remembering**

Next, you *store the new, understood information* in your memory. You remember some information longer than other information.

6. **Responding**

Being able to respond to what you hear proves that you understood it.

You respond to someone when you *ask questions*, *give your opinions*, and *use the new information* in your daily life.

Listening Myths

Some people have the wrong idea of what listening is. Each of the ideas below is a myth. None of the ideas are true. How many of these myths have you believed in the past?

Listening is hearing.

Just because your ears work doesn't mean you're a good listener. Remember, hearing is only the first step in listening.

I can't improve my listening skills.

Yes, you can! If you learn how to be a better listener and practice good listening, you *can* improve your listening skills.

If I'm a good reader, I'll be a good listener.

Listening and reading are two different skills. To be an effective listener, you have to work on listening skills, not reading skills.

It's the speaker's job to make me a good listener.

The speaker doesn't know if you understand his message or not. It's *your* responsibility to take an active part in listening. You have a choice about the kind of listener you want to be.

I'll become a better listener as I get older.

Listening skills improve with practice and effort, not with age!

Types of Listening

Type of Listening	Why You Use It	Examples
Appreciative	to listen for enjoyment	listening to music watching a movie or a play listening to a comedian
Empathic	to understand someone's feelings	listening to friends listening to someone whose opinions are different from yours listening to someone tell about a personal experience
Comprehensive	to listen for information	listening to your teachers, parents, and supervisors listening to directions listening to informational TV programs
Evaluative	to judge a message	listening to a TV commercial listening to a salesperson listening to anyone who's trying to persuade you

Why Do You Listen?

Name _____

List some reasons you should listen in each situation below. Then, give an example of a time you listened in each situation and how your good listening skills helped you.

1. at school _____

_____

_____

2. at home _____

_____

_____

3. on the job _____

_____

_____

4. at a play or concert _____

_____

_____

5. taking a phone message for someone _____

_____

_____

6. at a friend's house _____

_____

_____

Listen Up!

Name _____

Almost 50% of your communication time is spent listening. If you're a good listener, you won't miss directions or assignments. You won't have to ask people to repeat themselves.

Why would good listening be important in the following situations? Give at least two reasons for each item.

1. It's your first week at a new job. Your supervisor is training you to use a computerized cash register. _____

   _____

2. Your aunt calls to talk to your stepdad, who's not home. Your aunt decides to leave a message. _____

   _____

3. Your teacher announces which chapters and vocabulary words will be on the semester test.

   _____

   _____

4. Your best friend is upset about a fight he had with his girlfriend last night.

   _____

   _____

5. You're in charge of the props for your school theater production. The director has the cast run through Act I. _____

   _____

Listen Up!

Why would good listening be important in the following situations? Write your answers on the lines below.

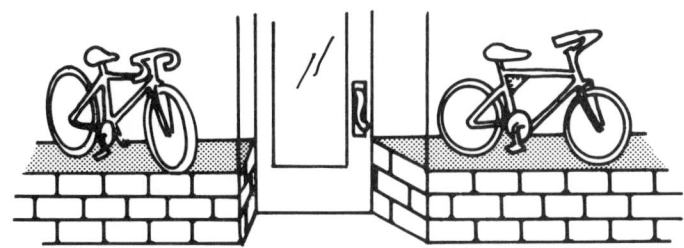

6. You've saved enough money to buy a bicycle. The store salesclerk is describing the features

    of three different bicycles. _____

    _____

7. You've been absent from school for a week. A friend brings you a week's worth of

    assignments and tells you what you've missed. _____

    _____

8. Your doctor is explaining what you should do for your flu symptoms. She writes you a

    prescription. _____

    _____

9. On Monday, your mom leaves on a business trip for a week. She lists the things you need

    to take care of while she's gone. _____

    _____

10. You're watching a mystery movie with your friends. _____

    _____

Teacher Tips

> Appreciative Listening, pages 34 and 35
> Empathic Listening, pages 36 to 40
> Comprehensive Listening, pages 41 to 43
> Evaluative Listening, pages 44 to 51

Do your students know how to distinguish among different kinds of listening? Do they know about the different listening skills they need? In this unit, your students will acquire the skills they need to listen effectively in different situations. Your students will learn that success in school, in personal relationships, and at work depends on their ability to listen.

They'll discover that listening can be done on a variety of levels. They'll learn that appreciative listeners listen for enjoyment. They'll learn how to be more empathic listeners who help their friends solve their problems. As comprehensive listeners, they'll learn to be more successful students. And they'll be informed decision makers after they understand what it means to be evaluative listeners.

Begin by reviewing the handout *Types of Listening* from Unit 1. Then, discuss the handouts and activity sheets from this unit. By the end of this unit, your students will know how to be good listeners in a variety of situations.

Handout: 5 Ways to Listen for Enjoyment

After discussing that appreciative listening is listening for enjoyment, your students will read about some suggestions for improving this type of listening. Reinforce the idea that appreciative listening is not time wasted!

Activity Sheet: As You Like It!

This activity will help your students identify their personal preferences for listening. Since each student is an individual with unique tastes, your students will discover that they enjoy listening to a variety of music, TV shows, radio stations, and sounds in nature.

Encourage your students to be honest as they share their preferences for the things they like to listen to. Don't hesitate to share your own tastes for appreciative listening!

Listening for Appreciation

Ask each student to listen to a musical recording at home or in the school library. Have them write down their thoughts and feelings as they listen. Then, ask volunteers to share what they wrote. Talk about how often your students listen for pleasure, the amount of time they spend listening, and what costs might be involved in listening for appreciation. Ask your students if they'd like to have more time to listen for appreciation. Finally, discuss the fact that appreciative listening is important because listening to music and nature for pleasure helps many people relax.

Handout: 9 Ways to Listen with Understanding

This handout explains what empathy means and offers your students specific ways to be understanding listeners. The strategies include listening without judging, using verbal and nonverbal feedback, and offering positive responses to friends and family.

As You Like It!   Name _____

Before you can *appreciate* the things you listen to, you have to know what things you *like* to listen to. Which types of listening do you like?

Give specific examples if you can. Then, compare your answers to the rest of the class.

1. **Recorded Performances**

    a. radio — specific shows or stations *Answers will vary.* _____

    b. music

rock _____		country _____
heavy metal _____		classical _____
progressive _____		jazz _____
rap _____		new age _____
Christian _____		easy listening _____

    c. bands _____

    d. talk shows _____

    e. drama shows _____

    f. comedy shows _____

2. **Live Performances**

    a. bands _____

    b. plays _____

    c. solo singers _____

    d. friends who entertain you _____

    e. comedy acts or performances _____

    f. musical theater performances _____

3. **Other** _____

Unit 2
Activity Sheet   35   125 Ways to Be a Better Listener
                                                                 Copyright © 1992 LinguiSystems, Inc.

Activity Sheet: I Hear You

Chances are, your students often want to understand their friends' feelings, but they can't always identify those feelings. Your students will use this activity sheet to learn how to be more empathic listeners. First, your students will describe feelings and emotions from hypothetical situations. Then, they'll rephrase negative responses to these feelings into responses that show more empathy. Encourage your students to talk about times when they wished someone had been more empathic with their feelings.

Listening to Be Empathic

Encourage your students to use the empathic listener strategies the next time they're listening to a friend's problem. Then, as a class, ask your students if they felt they were good listeners while listening to their friends. Did your students feel they better understood their friends' problems than before they learned about empathic listening? How do they plan to use empathic listening strategies in the future?

I Hear You　　　　　　　Name _____

Sometimes it's hard to know how other people feel. But if you can figure out how your friends feel, you'll be a better listener. You'll understand your friends and what they're going through.

Read the following situations. Describe how the speaker might be feeling. Then, change the negative responses into empathic responses. Use the first one as an example.

1. *Jane:* If I get one more homework assignment, I'm going to scream! I have too much to do this weekend. How am I ever going to get all of this done?

   Monica: Oh, Jane, you say that *every* week!

   How would you describe Jane's feelings? _frustrated, overwhelmed_

   To be a more empathic listener, Monica could have said: _Yeah, there's always too much_

   to do on the weekends. Maybe we can do some assignments together.

2. *Mitch:* Please ask him! The last time I asked for help, Mr. Lewis yelled at me! I think he's always mad at me for not understanding this geometry.

   Brad: You're such a chicken! Just raise your hand and do it!

   How would you describe Mitch's feelings? _embarrassed, intimidated, afraid_

   To be a more empathic listener, Brad could have said: _I know what you mean._

   Mr. Lewis can be impatient; have you talked to your counselor?

Unit 2　Activity Sheet　39　　125 Ways to Be a Better Listener　Copyright © 1992 LinguiSystems, Inc.

I Hear You　　　　　　　Name _____

3. *Grandmother:* You kids never come to see me anymore. All I do is sit here and grow old! It sure would be nice if I had some friends visit me.

   Grandson: What do you mean you wish you had friends? What about your neighbors?

   How would you describe the grandmother's feelings? _lonely, forgotten, sad_

   To be a more empathic listener, the grandson could have said: _I'll try to visit_

   you more often; maybe you could join a club.

4. *Travis:* I knew this would happen! My dad promised we'd go fishing this weekend, but now he's got to work again! He always breaks his promises.

   Natasha: Forget about it! What's so great about fishing anyway?

   How would you describe Travis' feelings? _neglected, unimportant, frustrated_

   To be a more empathic listener, Natasha could have said: _My parents can't do_

   everything they want to, either; have you told your dad how you feel?

5. *Lynn:* I'm so tired of hearing my parents argue. I wish they wouldn't talk to each other that way.

   Tai: It's no big deal. Most parents fight.

   How would you describe Lynn's feelings? _worried, angry, afraid_

   To be a more empathic listener, Tai could have said: _Remember, it's not your_

   fault they fight; do your parents know how you feel?

6. *Wesley:* Some people think I'm a baby for being so upset about my dog dying. But we had him for 10 years! It's really like losing a member of my family.

   George: Well, you'll forget about it soon. You can always get another dog.

   How would you describe Wesley's feelings? _sad, embarrassed, angry_

   To be a more empathic listener, George could have said: _I'm sorry your dog_

   died; some people don't understand how important a pet can be.

Unit 2　Activity Sheet　40　　125 Ways to Be a Better Listener　Copyright © 1992 LinguiSystems, Inc.

Handout: 6 Ways to Listen for Information

Most of the listening your students do during their day is comprehensive – they listen for information. In fact, all listening is a form of comprehensive listening. Read the first two paragraphs aloud. Then, discuss this handout with your students to help them become more successful at listening for information. Explain to your students that good comprehensive listeners are generally good students.

Activity Sheet: I Get It!

Have each student take the *I Get It!* activity sheet to his next academic class. Encourage him to answer the questions as he hears his teacher give the information. Then, have your students bring their completed activity sheets back to your class. Talk about the importance of focusing attention, asking questions, and listening for relevant information. Discuss the fact that listening becomes easier when you know what to listen for.

I Get It!　　　　　　Name _____

Read the questions below. Then, take this activity sheet with you to your next class, such as science, English, history, or math.

Answer the questions before, during, and after class to practice your comprehensive listening.

Before Class

1. What thoughts should I push from my head before I get to this class? _____

    Answers will vary. _____

2. What kind of information will I probably hear during this class? _____
    _____

During Class

3. What assignments or special announcements should I listen for? _____
    _____

4. How can I use all my senses? _____
    _____

5. What notes should I be taking? _____
    _____

6. What questions can I ask so the messages I heard make sense? _____
    _____
    _____

After Class

7. How can I prepare for the next time I come to this class? _____
    _____

Unit 2
Activity Sheet　　　　　43　　　　　125 Ways to Be a Better Listener
Copyright © 1992 LanguiSystems, Inc.

Listening for Comprehension

Read a newspaper article to your students. Tell them to listen carefully and take notes on the details they hear. Then, ask them questions about the article to determine how well they used their new skills.

Handout: 7 Ways to Evaluate a Message

Before you discuss the handout with your students, explain that they'll use these techniques as they listen to persuasive speeches, commercial advertisements, and sales pitches. Then, discuss the handout to help your students become more effective evaluative listeners.

Handout: 4 Ways to Evaluate Commercials

Your students probably hear lots of TV and radio commercials every day. Now that they know how to evaluate messages in general, they should probably learn how to evaluate commercials in particular. Adolescents are becoming a huge group of consumers. This handout will help them become better listeners *and* smart consumers.

Activity Sheet: What Do You Think?

Review the checklist from the *7 Ways to Evaluate a Message* handout (tip 27) with your students. Then, give each student four copies of the *What Do You Think?* activity sheet. You may prefer your students to work in groups of two or three to complete this activity.

Next, read the four passages on pages 48 and 49 to your students. After you read each passage, have your students complete an activity sheet. Discuss your students' answers when they're finished.

Listening for Evaluation

Do your students make good consumer decisions? Give each student three copies of the *What Do You Think?* activity sheet. Then, have him listen carefully to three TV or radio commercials and answer the questions on the sheet.

Finally, talk about the advertised items and whether or not your students would buy them.

How easily are your students persuaded by each other? Have each student give a three-minute persuasive speech on a topic, such as those listed below. Then, let her classmates discuss how persuasive she was. Use the questions from the *What Do You Think?* activity to guide the discussions.

- Dogs make better pets than cats.
- The best place for a vacation is _____.
- Smoking is very bad for your health.
- It's important to learn to say no.
- I'm the best person for the job. (name the job)
- Girls and boys should/should not play on the same school athletic teams.
- Dress codes should/should not be enforced at school.
- Boys and girls should/should not be required to complete a home economics course.
- School should/should not be in session all year round.
- Spring vacation should be lengthened/shortened.
- The food in the school cafeteria should/should not be catered by national chain restaurants.
- Foreign language courses should/should not be required in junior and senior high school.
- Sex education should/should not be provided in school.
- The age requirement for driving/drinking should be raised/lowered.

Activity Sheet: Listen to This

Let your students determine how well they recognize appreciative, empathic, comprehensive, and evaluative listening by completing the *Listen to This* activity sheet on page 51. Your students will read about a variety of listening situations and decide which kind of listening each situation requires.

Listen to This   Name _____

Use your handout from Unit 1, *Types of Listening*, to help you complete this activity. Read each situation below. Then, decide if you would use appreciative, empathic, comprehensive, or evaluative listening skills for each situation. Write your answer on the lines.

1. A political candidate is running for office. You're listening to a TV commercial that says you should vote for her. The candidate outlines five reasons why you should vote for her.

   evaluative

2. Your computer lab instructor is talking about a new program that you'll be using. He describes the different ways the program can be used.

   comprehensive

3. Your relatives have come to visit. Your cousin says he wants to talk to you about something personal. You go to a quiet part of the house to talk.

   empathic

4. A TV commercial urges you to order a collection of tapes. The commercial claims the tapes include all of the greatest hits of the '80's, and that you won't find a better collection in any music store.

   evaluative

5. You're in your living room. You decide to play a CD by your favorite group. You put on headphones so you can turn up the volume as loud as you want.

   appreciative

6. Your parents are leaving for the day and you'll be babysitting your younger brothers. Your parents tell you where you can reach them in case there's an emergency.

   comprehensive

7. Your stepdad listens to classical music when he's feeling down. He says the music puts him in a good mood.

   appreciative

8. A salesperson describes the "fantastic savings" you can receive on magazines if you order through United Publishers today.

   evaluative

Unit 2
Activity Sheet   51   125 Ways to Be a Better Listener
                                                        Copyright © 1992 LinguiSystems, Inc.

Additional Activities

Appreciative Listening

Have your students ask their friends and family members what types of listening they do for enjoyment. Are their choices for appreciative listening the same as your students' choices or different?

Encourage your students to take part in a listening experience they normally wouldn't choose to do. Ask them to listen with an open mind and then identify at least two reasons why someone might enjoy that listening experience.

Empathic Listening

Ask each student to write how he feels when someone doesn't listen empathically to him. Have each student tell about a time he felt a listener didn't use good empathic listening skills.

Have students volunteer to spend some time with your school's counselors. Have the students share the empathic listening handout with each counselor and find out which techniques each counselor uses. What types of responses do the counselors use most often? Do the counselors feel their empathic listening skills improve with practice?

Comprehensive Listening

Have your students watch a videotaped newscast during class. Ask them questions about the information they heard. Talk about which listening techniques they used as they listened.

Evaluative Listening

Have your students bring in examples of sweeping cause statements or emotional appeals they've heard or seen in advertising. Talk about the ads' claims and whether your students accept or reject the claims and why.

Encourage each student to analyze a recent purchase she has made. Have her consider the following questions.

> Why did I buy the item?
> Was I persuaded by an ad or commercial to buy this item?
> Am I satisfied with my purchase?
> Could I have made a more informed choice?
> Knowing what I know now about evaluative listening, would I still buy this item?

5 Ways to Listen for Enjoyment

When's the last time you listened to your favorite band? What sounds in nature do you enjoy? Which talk shows do you like? When you listen to something for enjoyment, you're listening for *appreciation*.

Appreciative listening is listening for pleasure. Try following the tips below. You'll find you appreciate music, talk shows, maybe the sounds of a crowded street even more!

1 **Think about the things you like to listen to.**

Everyone has his own likes and dislikes. Circle the types of listening you're interested in. Then, make the time to listen to the things you enjoy. Listening for entertainment is a good way to relax.

TV shows   radio   comedy performances
talk shows   singers   instrumental musicians
solo singers   concerts   theater performances
musical groups   music you perform   friends who are entertaining

2 **Listen for enjoyment by yourself.**

Spending time by yourself can be fun. Spend some time alone to gather your thoughts, unwind, or calm down after a hard day. You might watch a favorite TV show or listen to some music. Appreciative listening helps reduce stress because you're doing something you enjoy.

3 **Listen for enjoyment with other people.**

Go to a concert, sit on a street corner, or play tapes with a friend or two. You can learn a lot when you spend time with friends. For example, you might not understand what a song is about until a friend explains it to you. Plus, it's fun to spend time with people who like the same things you do.

4 **Let your friends choose music or TV shows they like.**

You and your friends might not like listening to the same things. So, you should take turns listening to each other's choices. Say you're riding in your friend's car and he turns up the radio volume to listen to a song you don't like. Don't say "How can you listen to that stuff. I hate that!" Instead, let your friend enjoy his music. You'll have a chance to listen to your selections later.

5 **Remember, the time you spend in appreciative listening isn't time wasted.**

Everyone needs to relax, and one way to relax is to listen to something you enjoy. If you haven't listened to something just for the fun of it lately, treat yourself! Let yourself listen to the things you like because *you* want to.

As You Like It!

Name _____

Before you can *appreciate* the things you listen to, you have to know what things you *like* to listen to. Which types of listening do you like?

Give specific examples if you can. Then, compare your answers to the rest of the class.

1. **Recorded Performances**

    a. radio — specific shows or stations _____

    b. music

    rock _____   country _____

    heavy metal _____   classical _____

    progressive _____   jazz _____

    rap _____   new age _____

    Christian _____   easy listening _____

    c. bands _____

    d. talk shows _____

    e. drama shows _____

    f. comedy shows _____

2. **Live Performances**

    a. bands _____

    b. plays _____

    c. solo singers _____

    d. friends who entertain you _____

    e. comedy acts or performances _____

    f. musical theater performances _____

3. **Other** _____

9 Ways to Listen with Understanding

Your friends often tell you about problems they have. When you listen to friends tell you their problems, you try to understand their feelings. When you listen to someone and try to understand what they're feeling, you're using *empathic* listening.

You can strengthen personal relationships if you improve your empathic listening skills because people like to spend time with someone who is a "good listener."

As an empathic listener, you'll learn more about people, their backgrounds, and their experiences. Social workers, counselors, "hot line" workers, and members of the clergy are usually very good empathic listeners.

By practicing the following tips, you should be able to improve your empathic listening skills.

6 **Listen without adding your own ideas about what your friend is feeling.**

In other words, keep your opinions to yourself. This can be difficult, especially if your friend's experiences or background is very different from your own. But remember, your friend needs someone to talk to. He's probably not very interested in your opinions at this time.

7 **Say your friend's name during the conversation.**

People like to hear their own names. When you're listening empathically to your friend, say her name as you respond to her.

For example, you might say, "You know, Teri, I've felt that way before" or "Emilio, I'm really sorry about your sad news."

8 **Keep your friend's point of view in mind.**

Ask yourself the following questions:

"What does this problem mean to my friend?"
"How does he see the problem?"
"What is he feeling?"

9 Ways to Listen with Understanding, *continued*

9   **Respond to your friend with words and actions.**

Empathic listeners make their friends feel safe and comfortable. You need to show your friend that you support her feelings. Then, she'll know you're really listening to her and that you think her feelings are important. Here are some good responses to let your friend know you're listening to her:

> Nod your head.
>
> Smile and show that you're concerned.
>
> Look at your friend.
>
> Don't fidget.
>
> Use a pleasant voice. Speak softly and slowly.
>
> Hug your friend if you think it's okay to do. Sometimes a hug is all your friend might need.
>
> Say "Yes," or "Uh-huh" every now and then. (But remember that too many "uh-huhs" can be annoying and distracting!)
>
> Repeat your friend's message so she knows you understand what she's saying.

10   **Encourage your friend to keep talking.**

What's a great way to get your friend to talk? Ask questions! Your questions will show your friend you're interested in what he's saying. Asking your friend questions can help him express his feelings.

But be careful not to ask too many questions or your friend might think you're being nosy or quizzing him. Here are some questions you might want to ask:

> "How did you feel then?"
>
> "What do you mean by . . . ?"
>
> "Why do you think he said that?"
>
> "What do you think you could do to . . . ?"
>
> "What part of that bothers you most?"
>
> "Are you more upset about . . . or . . . ?"

9 Ways to Listen with Understanding, *continued*

11   **Encourage your friend to solve her own problems.**

Don't tell your friend what *you* think she should do. Instead, let her talk through her problems. Then, help her come up with a solution. You can help your friend solve her problems if you use responses like:

"What are your choices?"
"Have you thought about any other plans?"
"What do you think you should do?"
"Maybe it would help to talk to . . ."

12   **Even if your friend has done something or said something you disapprove of, try not to show your disapproval.**

Your friend might become defensive or stop talking, and the reason he came to you in the first place is because he needs to talk. Try not to say things like:

"I can't believe you said that!"
"You're crazy if you . . ."
"How dumb can you be?"
"You know what your problem is, don't you?"
"I told you this would happen."
"That was a pretty stupid thing to do."

If you say things like this, you're being a judge instead of an empathic listener.

13   **Let your friend know that his feelings are acceptable.**

Your friend might be confused by his feelings. He might feel stupid or foolish for feeling a certain way. But your friend has a right to feel the way he does. Tell him it's okay for him to feel hurt, mad, upset, or afraid.

14   **Understand that you won't always know what to say or how to help your friends solve their problems.**

Sometimes, people just want someone to listen to them. They don't necessarily expect you to solve their problems.

Let your friends know that you understand their feelings. Even though you might not know what to say to help your friends, they'll feel better knowing that you're ready to listen.

I Hear You

Name _____

Sometimes it's hard to know how other people feel. But if you can figure out how your friends feel, you'll be a better listener. You'll understand your friends and what they're going through.

Read the following situations. Describe how the speaker might be feeling. Then, change the negative responses into empathic responses. Use the first one as an example.

1. *Jane*: If I get one more homework assignment, I'm going to scream! I have too much to do this weekend. How am I ever going to get all of this done?

   Monica: Oh, Jane, you say that *every* week!

   How would you describe Jane's feelings? _*frustrated, overwhelmed*_____

   To be a more empathic listener, Monica could have said: _*Yeah, there's always too much*_

   _*to do on the weekends; maybe we can do some assignments together.*_____

2. *Mitch*: Please ask him! The last time I asked for help, Mr. Lewis yelled at me! I think he's always mad at me for not understanding this geometry.

   Brad: You're such a chicken! Just raise your hand and do it!

   How would you describe Mitch's feelings? _____

   To be a more empathic listener, Brad could have said: _____

   _____

I Hear You

3. *Grandmother*: You kids never come to see me anymore. All I do is sit here and grow old! It sure would be nice if I had some friends visit me.

   Grandson: What do you mean you wish you had friends? What about your neighbors?

   How would you describe the grandmother's feelings? _____

   To be a more empathic listener, the grandson could have said: _____

   _____

4. *Travis*: I knew this would happen! My dad promised we'd go fishing this weekend, but now he's got to work again! He always breaks his promises.

   Natasha: Forget about it! What's so great about fishing anyway?

   How would you describe Travis' feelings? _____

   To be a more empathic listener, Natasha could have said: _____

   _____

5. *Lynn*: I'm so tired of hearing my parents argue. I wish they wouldn't talk to each other that way.

   Tai: It's no big deal. Most parents fight.

   How would you describe Lynn's feelings? _____

   To be a more empathic listener, Tai could have said: _____

   _____

6. *Wesley*: Some people think I'm a baby for being so upset about my dog dying. But we had him for 10 years! It's really like losing a member of my family.

   George: Well, you'll forget about it soon. You can always get another dog.

   How would you describe Wesley's feelings? _____

   To be a more empathic listener, George could have said: _____

   _____

6 Ways to Listen for Information

You may not realize it, but you spend a big part of your day listening for information. When you listen for information, you're using *comprehensive* listening skills. Your teachers give lectures and assignments, someone reads the daily announcements, the bus driver tells you which route to take, your parents ask you to help them with tasks – all these people are giving you information.

You need to have good comprehensive listening skills so you understand what you need to know and what you're expected to do.

What might happen if your comprehensive listening skills are poor? You might not complete an assignment or you might not follow directions. And worse, you might be told, "You weren't paying attention" or "You weren't listening."

Sometimes you don't do things because you didn't think you were *supposed* to do anything. The tips on these two pages will help you improve your comprehensive listening skills. The tips will help you understand the information you need to know.

15 Know when to use comprehensive listening.

It's important to know when you should use comprehensive listening. You need comprehensive listening skills whenever you need to understand something.

If you're in class and your teacher is lecturing, listen up. If you're a member of a team or a club, listen to the daily announcements.

If you're starting a new job, pay attention to your coworkers and supervisor; they have plenty of important information to tell you. If you're responsible for certain tasks at home, listen so you know when you're supposed to complete those tasks.

Remember, you're responsible for the information you're given during the day. Learn to listen for information that involves you.

16 Concentrate on the situation.

It might be hard to do, but it's important to pay attention when you're listening. Try not to think about Friday's basketball game while someone's giving you directions to her home. Don't worry about your girlfriend's birthday present during math class. Forget about the movie that's on TV tonight until *after* your dad tells you the grocery list.

If you concentrate on one thing at a time, you'll hear the information you need.

6 Ways to Listen for Information, *continued*

17   Use your five senses.

The more of your five senses you use to listen, the more you'll be able to remember what you heard. *Listen* to the speaker. *Look* at the speaker. *Write* notes. *Touch* any tools or instruments the speaker is explaining how to use.

If you use your senses of touch and sight along with your sense of hearing, you'll remember information longer.

18   Listen for important information.

Unfortunately, some messages include information that's not very important. You need to decide what information you need to listen to *at this moment*. While your mom is telling you when to pick your sister up at the day-care center, listen for the time you're supposed to be there. It doesn't matter that your mom can't do it because she has to go to work early. Listen for the information you need to understand the message.

19   Ask questions.

If you're confused by directions or if you don't understand what you're supposed to do, ask questions. If you're not sure you heard something right, ask the speaker to repeat what she said. Remember, it's up to you to get the information you need.

20   Repeat the message.

After someone has given you directions, repeat the directions to him. If your supervisor gives you three tasks she wants done by noon, repeat the list of tasks to her.

Repeating a message gives the speaker the chance to say either, "Yes, that's right" or "No, that's not what I meant." Then the speaker can tell you her message in a different way.

I Get It!

Name _____

Read the questions below. Then, take this activity sheet with you to your next class, such as science, English, history, or math.

Answer the questions before, during, and after class to practice your comprehensive listening.

Before Class

1. What thoughts should I push from my head before I get to this class? _____

   _____

2. What kind of information will I probably hear during this class? _____

   _____

During Class

3. What assignments or special announcements should I listen for? _____

   _____

4. How can I use all my senses? _____

   _____

5. What notes should I be taking? _____

   _____

6. What questions can I ask so the messages I heard make sense? _____

   _____

   _____

After Class

7. How can I prepare for the next time I come to this class? _____

   _____

7 Ways to Evaluate a Message

When is the last time someone tried to convince you of something? While you listened to that person, you were probably deciding to accept or reject what he was saying. That's what *evaluative* listeners do. They listen to a message and decide if they believe the message or not.

As an evaluative listener, you'll listen to the facts the speaker presents. You'll also decide how truthful you think the speaker is. Then, you'll use your own experiences to judge the speaker's message. You'll decide if you agree with what the speaker is saying.

Some examples of claims you need to evaluate are:

Ms. DeSmet is a better guidance counselor than Ms. Loras.
You should go to the game on Friday night. It'll be fun.
State taxes must be raised if we want to pay for road repair.
Male students who wear earrings are troublemakers.
Girls don't play basketball as well as boys.

Here's a list of ways to help you become a better evaluative listener.

21   Think about the information you've heard.

Can the information be proved? Decide if the information is:

a fact – statements that can be proved.
an opinion – statements of personal feelings that can't be proved or disproved.
a statistic – numerical data that can be proved.

Before you judge a message, ask yourself if it can be proved. If something can't be proved, you need to decide if you'll accept it or not.

22   Decide if you can trust the information.

Find out if the information is dependable. Ask:

"Is the information current?"
"Does the information make sense?"
"Are there enough examples?"
"Do I know where the information came from?"

If you answer "no" to any of these questions, you might want to reject the information.

7 Ways to Evaluate a Message, *continued*

23 Learn to pick out opinions that sound like facts.

Some opinions sound like facts. Listen for phrases such as:

"I heard that . . ."
"We know that . . ."
"It's reported that . . ."
"They say that . . ."
"My brother knows a guy who said that . . ."

If you hear phrases like these, you need to ask some questions. Ask these people *where* they heard their information, exactly *who* said something, and *where* something is reported. Even if you agree with these statements, ask questions to determine if they're true.

24 Listen to the whole message before you make your decision.

Don't tune out a message half way through. Listen to the entire message and try to understand what the speaker is saying. Then, decide if you believe the message or not.

25 If you're not sure you can judge a message, ask questions.

Ask the speaker to clear up any confusing statements she's made. Ask the speaker to give you another example. If the speaker can't or won't answer your questions, you need to decide if you have enough information to make a decision.

26 Understand that different people respond differently to the same message.

Your reaction to a message might be different from your friends' reactions. Maybe your mood, your background, or your experiences tell you to accept or reject a message. Your friends may disagree with your decision. But remember, it's important for everyone to react in his own way.

27 Decide to accept or reject the speaker's message.

Go through the following checklist while you listen to the whole message:

✓ What is the point of the message?
✓ Do I believe the speaker and trust him?
✓ Are there enough examples?
✓ Is the information an opinion or a fact?
✓ Have all of my questions been answered?

After some practice, you'll be able to answer these questions quickly. You'll become a good evaluative listener who makes good judgments.

4 Ways to Evaluate Commercials

You probably hear *lots* of TV and radio commercials every day. As a consumer, you need to listen closely to commercials.

You need to decide if you believe what the commercial is telling you. Mostly, you need to decide if you'll buy something or not.

These four tips will help you make your decisions.

28   Beware of tricky advertising.

Commercials can be sneaky in the way they present products. The list below shows some examples of commercials that you need to evaluate closely.

bandwagon   *People who eat potato chips prefer Mr. Chips. Buy Mr. Chips today!*

The claim is that other people do something or buy something, so you should, too.

scarcity   *Only 20 more Rebus trucks are left on our lot. Hurry down to buy yours at great savings while the supply lasts!*

The ad says to buy an item because there only a few left. Ask yourself if you really need the item.

authority   *This is Judy Gymnast. I use Deep Red Heat ointment to soothe my sore muscles. I bet it will work on your tired muscles, too.*

Advertisers often use celebrities or authority figures, like doctors and athletes, to sell their products. Having a celebrity speak about a product doesn't mean it works or that it's right for you.

29   Listen for emotional appeals.

Some commercials try to convince you by speaking to your emotions. The speakers in the commercials hope you will respond with your feelings rather than with your good sense. Emotional appeals can take the following forms:

If you want to be beautiful like me, use this shampoo.

If you want to have fun, buy a four-wheel drive truck.

People who want to make lots of money work for us. You should, too.

Emotional statements speak to your dreams, your needs, and your fears. If you recognize emotional appeals, you'll see that someone is trying to persuade you to buy something. Be sure you carefully evaluate the commercial before you decide to buy anything.

4 Ways to Evaluate Commercials, *continued*

30 **Be aware of sweeping cause statements.**

Sweeping cause statements are used a lot in commercials. These statements claim that *A* causes *B*, without considering other things that may cause *B* to happen. For example, someone might say "One hundred women who used Nu-Glow Moisturizer for 30 days looked younger."

This statement claims that using Nu-Glow Moisturizer caused the women to look younger. But ask yourself if anything else, such as changing climate, stopping smoking, or using makeup, could have made the women look younger.

31 **Decide if you can trust the speaker.**

If a person who breeds dogs tells you which cat food is best, can you trust that person? Ask yourself, "What does this person know about cat food? Is he an authority on cats or cat food? Do I think he's trustworthy?"

It's important to decide if you trust the person who's trying to sell you something. Don't be fooled into buying something just because the speaker is famous, or because he has a fancy title, or because he looks nice.

What Do You Think?

Read each paragraph to your students. Be sure to tell them the source of each paragraph. Then, have your students answer the questions on the *What Do You Think?* activity sheet.

When your students are finished, discuss their answers and analyze the persuasiveness of each paragraph.

A. TV commercial

Hi! You may recognize me. I'm Joe Player, linebacker for the Chicago Bears. Many of my fans ask me, "Joe, how'd you get to be so strong?" Well, it's no secret – I drink two Pump-Up Power drinks every day. For breakfast and again for lunch, I mix Pump-Up Power with milk and the results are obvious! The special formula gives me what I need for strength, energy, and muscle development. So, don't just wish you looked like me – do it! Try Pump-Up Power today – for a new you!

B. local pediatrician speaking to an elementary school PTA

Good evening. My name is Dr. Angel Martin. I have been a pediatrician for 12 years. This evening I'll tell you why children should go to bed by 7:30.

First of all, children who get plenty of sleep are better rested the next day. It's obvious that students learn more if they're well rested. Second, if children get to bed early, they won't waste time watching TV. Everyone knows that watching TV is bad for children. Third, I think that children who get plenty of sleep are healthier than children who don't get enough sleep. Better health means fewer absences. Children who are seldom absent are good students.

I believe you parents want the best for your children – otherwise you wouldn't be here. So if you want to be the best parents to your children, you should put them to bed by 7:30.

C. speech presented by a student

Living in the city is better than living in the country. City life is more exciting because there's more to do. People who live in the city can go to theaters, zoos, museums, parks, and restaurants. You could go somewhere different every night of the week!

Another reason city life is better than rural life is that it's easy to get around in the city. All you have to do is jump on a bus, on a train, on a subway, or in a taxi! A final reason living in the city is better than living in the country is the shopping scene. In a city, you can go to all kinds of department stores and specialty shops. You can find anything you want in a big city. There's more to do in the city than there is in the country.

D.   speech presented by a parent to a school board

Please don't vote "yes" for making our students attend school on Saturdays. If students attend school six days a week, they'll have one less day to rest. Growing students need lots of rest. They need time to recover from the previous week. They also need time to take it easy before they begin the next week. Plus, if our children attend school on Saturdays, they'll probably have more homework, but one less day to work on it. Children have enough homework already.

Another reason school on Saturday is a bad idea is that students will have less time for extracurricular activities and less time to spend with their families. Activities outside of school are important, too! I hope you'll vote against the proposal to lengthen the school week.

What Do You Think?

Name _____

Listen as your teacher reads four passages that try to persuade you to do something. As you listen, refer to tip 27 on page 45 from your *7 Ways to Evaluate a Message* handout.

After you've listened to each passage, answer the questions below.

1. What is the speaker's claim? _____

_____

2. Do you trust the speaker? Why or why not? _____

_____

3. What examples did the speaker give to support his claim? _____

_____

4. Were the examples opinions or facts? _____

5. Do you think the speaker gave enough examples? Why or why not? _____

_____

_____

6. Can you trust the examples? Why or why not? _____

_____

7. Did the speaker appeal to your emotions? If so, how? _____

_____

8. What other information would you like to have? _____

_____

9. Do you accept or reject the speaker's claim? Why? _____

_____

Listen to This

Use your handout from Unit 1, *Types of Listening*, to help you complete this activity. Read each situation below. Then, decide if you would use appreciative, empathic, comprehensive, or evaluative listening skills for each situation. Write your answer on the lines.

1. A political candidate is running for office. You're listening to a TV commercial that says you should vote for her. The candidate outlines five reasons why you should vote for her.

   _____

2. Your computer lab instructor is talking about a new program that you'll be using. He describes the different ways the program can be used.

   _____

3. Your relatives have come to visit. Your cousin says he wants to talk to you about something personal. You go to a quiet part of the house to talk.

   _____

4. A TV commercial urges you to order a collection of tapes. The commercial claims the tapes include all of the greatest hits of the '80's, and that you won't find a better collection in any music store.

   _____

5. You're in your living room. You decide to play a CD by your favorite group. You put on headphones so you can turn up the volume as loud as you want.

   _____

6. Your parents are leaving for the day, and you'll be babysitting your younger brothers. Your parents tell you where you can reach them in case there's an emergency.

   _____

7. Your stepdad listens to classical music when he's feeling down. He says the music puts him in a good mood.

   _____

8. A salesperson describes the "fantastic savings" you can receive on magazines if you order through United Publishers today.

   _____

Teacher Tips

Now that your students are aware of different kinds of listening and the importance of listening in various situations, it's time for them to take the next step — getting ready to listen. This unit will help your students get into the right frame of mind, setting the stage for successful listening.

Your students will learn about *Listening Attention Levels (LAL)*. An LAL is the amount of attention your students need to listen in any given situation. They'll identify things that can distract them from listening and discover ways to eliminate those distractions. They'll explore ways to focus their attention. Finally, your students will learn how to develop and maintain a positive attitude toward listening.

As you and your students explore this unit, encourage them to carefully consider their own needs as they get ready to listen. Some students may need to work on their listening attitudes while others may need to deal with distractions.

By the end of this unit, your students will understand how to adjust their LALs, deal with distractions, focus their attention, and have a positive attitude toward listening. In other words, they'll be ready to listen!

Handout: 5 Tips About Your Listening Attention Level (LAL)

Read the first two paragraphs of this handout to your students. The term *Listening Attention Level (LAL)* is introduced as a way for your students to measure how much attention they need to pay in different situations. The handout explains that each student must exercise some conscious control over her attention. You may want to draw an LAL scale on the board as you explain that *0* represents *low attention* needed for listening and *5* represents *high attention* needed for listening.

Activity Sheet: Low Attention or High Attention?

This activity helps your students identify what LALs they need in different situations. Be sure to reinforce individual responses, validating personal estimates even if they're different from other students' responses. At the same time, discuss the need for questioning LALs.

For example, a student might believe he needs a low LAL for listening to a history lecture. Help the student think of reasons he may need to raise his LAL in this situation. Finally, discuss the LALs your students think are necessary for appreciative, empathic, comprehensive, and evaluative listening.

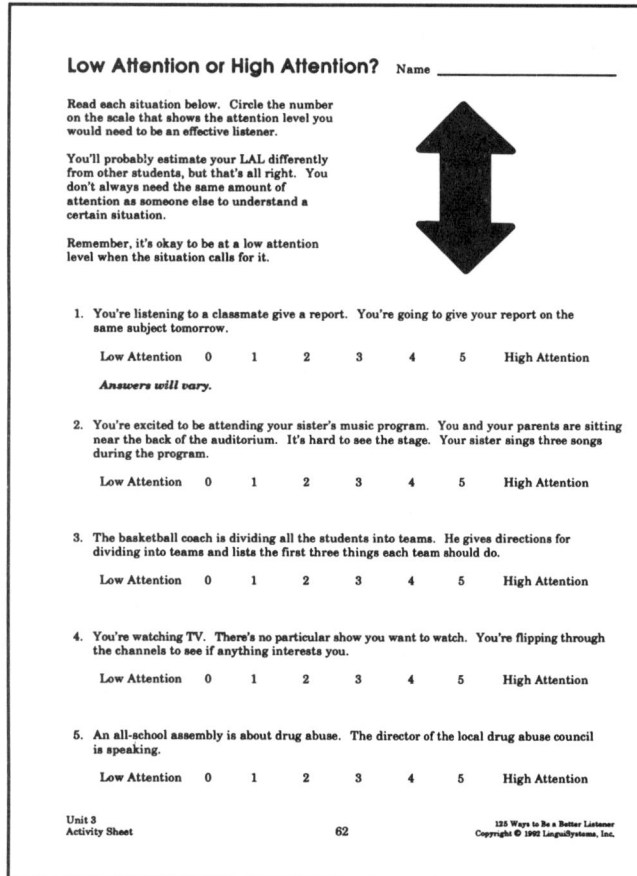

Low Attention or High Attention?   Name _____

Read each situation below. Circle the number on the scale that shows the attention level you would need to be an effective listener.

You'll probably estimate your LAL differently from other students, but that's all right. You don't always need the same amount of attention as someone else to understand a certain situation.

Remember, it's okay to be at a low attention level when the situation calls for it.

1. You're listening to a classmate give a report. You're going to give your report on the same subject tomorrow.

   Low Attention   0   1   2   3   4   5   High Attention

   Answers will vary.

2. You're excited to be attending your sister's music program. You and your parents are sitting near the back of the auditorium. It's hard to see the stage. Your sister sings three songs during the program.

   Low Attention   0   1   2   3   4   5   High Attention

3. The basketball coach is dividing all the students into teams. He gives directions for dividing into teams and lists the first three things each team should do.

   Low Attention   0   1   2   3   4   5   High Attention

4. You're watching TV. There's no particular show you want to watch. You're flipping through the channels to see if anything interests you.

   Low Attention   0   1   2   3   4   5   High Attention

5. An all-school assembly is about drug abuse. The director of the local drug abuse council is speaking.

   Low Attention   0   1   2   3   4   5   High Attention

Unit 3
Activity Sheet   62   125 Ways to Be a Better Listener
                                                    Copyright © 1992 LinguiSystems, Inc.

Low Attention or High Attention?   Name _____

6. Your Spanish teacher is reviewing for next week's test. She's going through four chapters in the book, pointing out information which may be on the test.

   Low Attention   0   1   2   3   4   5   High Attention

7. At your family reunion, your cousin is telling your parents what she's been doing the last two years. You've been visiting your cousin for a week and you already know her news.

   Low Attention   0   1   2   3   4   5   High Attention

8. You're babysitting for your neighbors. Before the parents leave, they tell you where they can be reached, when the children should be in bed, and where some snacks are.

   Low Attention   0   1   2   3   4   5   High Attention

9. You're on the phone with a friend. You're talking about what's been happening since you last spoke three days ago. Your baby sister is in the room, laughing and playing.

   Low Attention   0   1   2   3   4   5   High Attention

10. You're in your homeroom listening to the morning announcements. The speaker has already announced when the Spanish Club, which you're a member of, will meet. The speaker continues with the rest of the announcements.

   Low Attention   0   1   2   3   4   5   High Attention

Unit 3
Activity Sheet   63   125 Ways to Be a Better Listener
                                                    Copyright © 1992 LinguiSystems, Inc.

Handout: 7 Ways to Change Your LAL

In this handout, your students will learn how to raise or lower their LALs when going from one listening activity to another. After discussing the handout, ask your students which of the tips they've used in the past and how well the tips worked for them.

Activity: Make a Change!

Not only should your students learn how to estimate a needed LAL, but they should also learn how to change an LAL. This activity provides your students with exercises to do just that.

First, draw an LAL scale, like the ones on the *Low Attention or High Attention?* activity sheet, on the chalkboard. Next, for each listening situation on pages 65 and 66, read part *a* to your students. Have each student use the scale to write the LAL she thinks she needs for part *a*.

Then, read part *b*, and have each student write the LAL she needs for part *b*. Finally, discuss what your students would do to adjust their LALs as they progress from the listening activity in part *a* to the listening activity in part *b*.

Listening Activity: Determining LALs

Have each student keep a log of his LALs for the next three days. Encourage your students to determine the LAL for each listening activity they're engaged in and decide when their LAL needs to change. Let your students share their "research" with one another. Were your students more aware of their LALs after completing this section?

Handout: 8 Ways to Identify Distractions

This handout provides your students with strategies to identify potential listening distractions. Discuss the meaning of *distraction* and ask your students to tell about the things that distract them. Encourage your students to ask themselves the questions on the handout to determine whether or not something is a distraction.

Activity Sheet: What's Distracting You?

This activity encourages your students to think about the types of stimuli that distract them from listening effectively. You may want to have the students complete the activity sheet on their own and then share their answers in a group discussion.

The discussion will help your students learn about the things that are distracting for their peers and discover other distractions they may have overlooked.

Activity Sheet: That's Distracting!

Your students will have an opportunity to identify potential distractions within the context of four listening situations. Ask your students to underline the distractions in each situation. You'll probably get a variety of answers.

When your students have completed the activity sheet, have them explain how each underlined distraction might interfere with good listening.

What's Distracting You?   Name _____

What are some things that get in the way of your listening? Write examples of the things that distract you. Then, share your answers with your classmates. Can you help each other avoid some distractions?

1. things you see: *friends outside your classroom, cars outside a window, classmates*

    passing notes _____

2. things you hear: *Answers will vary.* _____

    _____

3. things about the room: _____

    _____

4. how you feel physically: _____

    _____

5. how you feel emotionally: _____

    _____

6. things about the speaker: _____

    _____

7. things about your attitude toward listening: _____

    _____

Unit 3
Activity Sheet   69   125 Ways to Be a Better Listener
                                          Copyright © 1992 LinguiSystems, Inc.

That's Distracting!   Name _____

Underline the possible distractions in each situation below. Use your *8 Ways to Identify Distractions* handout to complete each passage.

1. I went to a play with my stepmom last week. We were late, so I didn't get to eat beforehand. The theater had been built recently and the smell of fresh paint was still pretty strong. But the walls were beautiful! Each wall had a different scene from a famous play painted on it. I couldn't stop looking at them.

    The whole evening would have been enjoyable, except that the air conditioner droned the whole time.

2. Last Thanksgiving, my grandfather told us about his experiences during the war. Grandpa, who's hard of hearing, spoke very loudly as he told us his stories. My mom listened from the kitchen while my dad cleared the table. The rest of us sat in the living room. My two brothers kept poking each other while Grandpa talked.

    I thought Grandpa's stories were interesting and I learned some things I'd never known before. Eventually, my leg fell asleep because I was sitting cross-legged on the floor.

3. Nate went to school yesterday even though he woke up with a sore throat. He wanted to go to school because he was having a test in third period American Literature.

    In first period algebra, his teacher reviewed some concepts from chapter three. Several biology students were conducting a sulfur experiment in the classroom next door to Nate's.

    Toward the end of first period, Nate began to feel hot and wondered if he was getting a fever.

4. The Young Journalists Club had a guest speaker last week. The speaker is an editor of the local newspaper and he spoke about the responsibilities of his job. Every member of the club showed up. It was crowded in the small room.

    The editor knew a lot about the newspaper business, but his voice was hoarse and he coughed a lot. It didn't help that the club met next to the teachers' lounge where delivery men were stacking boxes.

    The meeting was held after school and it lasted an hour longer than most members thought it would. At least the speaker had a lot of interesting things to say.

Unit 3
Activity Sheet   70   125 Ways to Be a Better Listener
                                          Copyright © 1992 LinguiSystems, Inc.

Unit 3   56   125 Ways to Be a Better Listener

Handout: 4 Ways to Get Rid of Distractions

The last handout gave your students strategies for *identifying* distractions. Now your students will learn ways to *eliminate* them.

The strategies in this handout should be done in sequence. You may find it helpful to list these key words that identify each strategy on the chalkboard.

1. *Identify*   3. *Change*
2. *Ask*   4. *Set Aside*

Encourage your students to use the sequence of strategies to help them get rid of distractions.

For the concept of *set aside*, encourage your students to use visualization. For example, help them visualize their distracting thoughts about the big game tonight leaving their minds, floating quickly and quietly over to the shelf, and staying there while they listen to their math teacher introduce a new concept.

After completing the handout, you can reinforce what your students learn by having them use the key words *identify*, *ask*, *change*, and *set aside* when they need to focus on eliminating distractions in your classroom. In addition, you can model the skills your students have learned.

For example, as a transition to a lesson you might say, "I'm going to close the door because I'm having trouble hearing what you're saying" or "I'm excited to hear about that! Now I need to *set aside* that idea so I can focus on what we're going to talk about today."

Listening Activity: Eliminating Distractions

Have your students get into groups of two or three and brainstorm ways they can eliminate the distractions they listed on their *What's Distracting You?* activity sheets. Then, let each group share its eliminating strategies with each other. Finally, ask the following questions to encourage discussion among your students:

Tell about a time when you were distracted. What did you do to get rid of the distraction?

Tell about a time when you could have gotten rid of a distraction but you didn't. Why didn't you get rid of the distraction?

Tell about a distraction you didn't think you could get rid of. Tell how you might deal with this distraction if it happened again.

Handout: 5 Ways to Pay Attention

The strategies in this handout will help your students focus their attention during listening. After your students have had time to discuss the strategies, talk about the importance of focusing attention. Ask your students to tell you the disadvantages of not focusing attention in school, at home, and at work.

Activity: Coming Into Focus

Your students can use this activity sheet to practice the strategies from the *5 Ways to Pay Attention* handout. First, each student will choose a listening situation. Then, he'll practice paying attention in that situation by answering the questions on the activity sheet.

Ask your students to share their experiences with each other. Did they think it was easy to pay attention after following the tips on the handout?

Handout: 8 Ways to Have a Positive Listening Attitude

This handout provides eight ways for your students to take charge of their listening attitudes. After discussing the handout, encourage your students to share experiences they've had with having a positive or negative listening attitude.

Share examples of situations in which *you've* had a negative or positive attitude toward listening and the consequences of having each attitude. Be sure to suggest ways your negative attitude was changed or could have been changed to a positive attitude.

Activity Sheet: Go for the Positive!

In this activity, listening situations and a listener's negative attitude are described. For each situation, your students will change the negative attitude to a positive attitude. Then, they'll identify at least one possible outcome of listening effectively. Discuss your students' answers when they're finished.

Go for the Positive!   Name _____

Read the following situations. Change each negative attitude to a positive one. Then, give at least one positive outcome that might result from listening well.

1. Your best friend asks you to attend a poetry reading by her favorite poet. You first thought is, "I hate poetry!"

   Positive attitude: *"I've never been to a poetry reading, it might be interesting."*

   Positive outcome: *learn about poetry, have something else in common with your friend, appreciate poetry*

2. You've been assigned to listen to a radio talk show. The host, an ex-police officer, is talking about youth gangs. The host has an unusual voice and you disagree with the first two points he makes. You think, "This guy is crazy! What does he know about gangs anyway?"

   Positive attitude: *"This guy probably knows more about gangs than I do."*

   Positive outcome: *able to discuss the show in class tomorrow, hear a different point of view about gangs*

3. You're at an all-school assembly to hear campaign speeches from candidates for Student Senate. You're thinking, "I really don't care about this stuff!"

   Positive attitude: *"This year's candidates sound promising"; "I'll listen so I can make a good choice when I vote."*

   Positive outcome: *be an informed voter, learn which candidates are best for you and your school*

Unit 3
Activity Sheet   76   125 Ways to Be a Better Listener
Copyright © 1992 LinguiSystems, Inc.

Go for the Positive!   Name _____

4. Your volleyball team lost a match today. The coach is beginning one of her lectures. You think, "So what if we lost again! All this talking isn't going to make us a winning team!"

   Positive attitude: *"Coach takes practice seriously. Maybe she has some pointers today."*

   Positive outcome: *learn some strategies, understand your coach's point of view*

5. During Cultural Awareness Week, a guest speaker from Brazil comes to speak to your class. You're thinking, "Didn't we just finish a unit on Brazil? What's this speaker going to be able to teach us?"

   Positive attitude: *"It will be great to get a real account of life in Brazil."*

   Positive outcome: *hear viewpoint of someone who lives in Brazil, learn first-hand about a different culture*

6. You're serving on a committee to plan the Valentine's Day dance. The chairperson suggests you wear a heart costume to sell tickets tomorrow. You say to yourself, "No way! Where did she come up with that idea?"

   Positive attitude: *"It's a weird idea, but it could be fun. Maybe I'll make a green heart!"*

   Positive outcome: *sell tickets, avoid arguing with the chairperson*

7. You're watching a film about volcanoes in science class. You think, "This is so boring. Wake me when it's over."

   Positive attitude: *"I don't know much about volcanoes, but I wonder what causes them to erupt."*

   Positive outcome: *learn about volcanoes, be able to participate in a discussion about volcanoes*

Unit 3
Activity Sheet   77   125 Ways to Be a Better Listener
Copyright © 1992 LinguiSystems, Inc.

Additional Activities

★ Let each student write his description of an effective speaker. How does each student think a speaker can help eliminate distractions that prevent his audience from listening?

★ Let your students help each other become more effective listeners. Have a class discussion about the things that distract each student from listening. Then, ask your students to write and sign a class pledge promising to help each other listen.

★ Give your students the opportunity to apply what they've learned about distractions. Set up some distractions in your room, like turning a radio on or leaving a door open. If no one tries to eliminate the distraction, model the strategy for handling it yourself. Some examples are "After I shut this door, I'll be ready to listen to what you're saying" or "The sun in my eyes keeps me from paying attention. Let me close these curtains."

★ Have your students think about an experience they've had listening to a lecture or sermon. Ask them to tell what kind of attitude they had when they began to listen. Were they looking forward to listening? Did their attitude change as they listened?

★ Discuss how negative attitudes can get in the way of having a good listening and learning experience. Then, have each student think back to her class schedule at the beginning of the school year. Was there a class she was sure would be boring, but that she ended up enjoying? Talk about the need to keep an open mind about a variety of subjects and holding judgment until something is actually experienced.

5 Tips About Your Listening Attention Level (LAL)

Do you need to pay more attention to a radio commercial or to a documentary program? When you're in the hallways between classes, do you need to pay more or less attention than when you're in class? The amount of energy you need to pay attention is called your *Listening Attention Level*, or *LAL*.

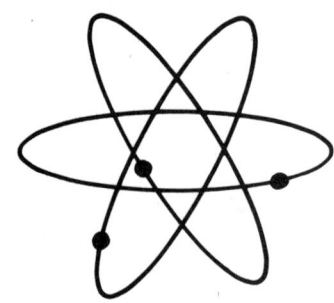

Good listeners know that some listening situations need more attention than others. They can figure out the LAL they need for each listening situation.

Here are some tips about your *LAL*.

32 **Imagine a scale from 0 to 5. 0 stands for low attention needed for listening, and 5 stands for high attention needed for listening.**

Low Attention   0   1   2   3   4   5   High Attention

If you don't need to pay a lot of attention in a situation, such as walking between classes, your attention level will be toward the low end of the scale.

If you need to work very hard to listen to something, such as listening in class, your attention level will be toward the high end of the scale.

33 **Be aware of your current LAL.**

Ask yourself, "How much energy do I need to pay attention right now? Am I on the low end of the scale, the high end of the scale, or somewhere in between? Should my LAL be higher or lower than it is, or is it just right?" On the LAL scale below, where are you right now?

Low Attention   0   1   2   3   4   5   High Attention

5 Tips About Your Listening Attention Level (LAL), *continued*

34 **Recognize that different LALs are needed at different times.**

For some activities, like listening to a friend's problem or walking across a busy street, you need a high LAL because there are important things to listen for in these situations. But for other activities, like attending a concert or writing an essay, a very low LAL is all you need.

35 **Ask questions about the listening activity you're getting ready for.**

If you're going from one listening activity to another, like going from lunch to your science class, ask yourself, "What am I going to listen to? What is the purpose of my listening? Who am I going to listen to?"

36 **Decide what LAL you'll need for the new listening situation.**

Ask yourself what LAL you needed the last time you were in a similar listening situation. Decide what LAL you'll need to pay attention this time.

Low Attention or High Attention? Name _____

Read each situation below. Circle the number on the scale that shows the attention level you would need to be an effective listener.

You'll probably estimate your LAL differently from other students, but that's all right. You don't always need the same amount of attention as someone else to understand a certain situation.

Remember, it's okay to be at a low attention level when the situation calls for it.

1. You're listening to a classmate give a report. You're going to give your report on the same subject tomorrow.

   Low Attention   0   1   2   3   4   5   High Attention

2. You're excited to be attending your sister's music program. You and your parents are sitting near the back of the auditorium. It's hard to see the stage. Your sister sings three songs during the program.

   Low Attention   0   1   2   3   4   5   High Attention

3. The basketball coach is dividing all the students into teams. He gives directions for dividing into teams and lists the first three things each team should do.

   Low Attention   0   1   2   3   4   5   High Attention

4. You're watching TV. There's no particular show you want to watch. You're flipping through the channels to see if anything interests you.

   Low Attention   0   1   2   3   4   5   High Attention

5. An all-school assembly is about drug abuse. The director of the local drug abuse council is speaking.

   Low Attention   0   1   2   3   4   5   High Attention

Low Attention or High Attention? Name _____

6. Your Spanish teacher is reviewing for next week's test. She's going through four chapters in the book, pointing out information that might be on the test.

    Low Attention   0   1   2   3   4   5   High Attention

7. At your family reunion, your cousin is telling your parents what she's been doing the last two years. You've been visiting your cousin for a week and you already know her news.

    Low Attention   0   1   2   3   4   5   High Attention

8. You're babysitting for your neighbors. Before the parents leave, they tell you where they can be reached, when the children should be in bed, and where some snacks are.

    Low Attention   0   1   2   3   4   5   High Attention

9. You're on the phone with a friend. You're talking about what's been happening since you last spoke three days ago. Your baby sister is in the room, laughing and playing.

    Low Attention   0   1   2   3   4   5   High Attention

10. You're in your homeroom listening to the morning announcements. The speaker has already announced when the Spanish Club, which you're a member of, will meet. The speaker continues with the rest of the announcements.

    Low Attention   0   1   2   3   4   5   High Attention

7 Ways to Change Your LAL

Now you know what a listening attention level is. You also know that different situations call for different LALs.

The tips in this handout will help you change your LAL. You'll be ready for any listening activity!

37   Decide if you need to change your LAL.

Ask yourself, "Do I need to change my current LAL to get ready for the new situation? How much of a change will I need to make?"

38   Raise your LAL if necessary by changing your posture.

Sit up straight in your chair, put both feet on the floor, and raise your head off your shoulders. Making a physical change can give you more energy to pay attention.

39   Raise your LAL by taking a quick, deep breath.

Take quick, deep breaths often while you listen, especially if you feel your attention level dropping. A deep breath fills your lungs with oxygen. Getting a burst of oxygen will give you a burst of energy.

40   Raise your LAL by facing the speaker.

It's easier to pay attention to someone when you're facing him. Study the speaker's facial expressions and gestures. A speaker's movements often give clues about what he's saying.

41   Raise your LAL by moving closer to the speaker, if possible.

Often if you're near the person who's talking, you can pay better attention. This is especially true in a large room. Sit close to the speaker so you can concentrate on his message.

42   Lower your LAL by taking a slow, deep breath.

The results of this technique are the opposite of number 39. Taking a long, deep breath then exhaling slowly helps you relax into a lower LAL.

43   Lower your LAL by relaxing your posture.

You don't need to pay a lot of attention in every situation. Sometimes, a relaxed posture and a low LAL can actually help you listen more closely. It helps to be in a relaxed mood when you're listening to something for the fun of it. Try it the next time you're listening to friends or enjoying music.

Make a Change!

Each situation I'm going to read has two parts. After I read the first part, write down your listening attention level from 0 to 5. Then, I'll read the second part of the situation. Decide what your listening attention for the second part should be and write it down.

When you're finished, we'll talk about the listening attention levels you chose.

1. a. You've just come out of gym class where you played a tiring game of volleyball. What is your LAL when you come out of gym class?

    b. You're going to math class where you'll be going over last night's homework assignment. What LAL will you need for math class?

2. a. In social studies class, you're listening to a lecture. You've taken two pages of notes so far. What is your LAL in social studies class?

    b. After social studies, you're in the hallway, heading to home economics. What is your LAL as you walk to home economics?

3. a. You're watching TV as you relax after school. What is your LAL as you watch TV?

    b. Your friend comes over to work with you on a project for the Science Fair. What is your LAL while you work on the project?

4. a. You and your family are at the airport, waiting for a plane to arrive. The announcer is listing the incoming flights and their gate numbers. What is your LAL as you listen to the announcement?

    b. Aaron, a foreign exchange student, has just arrived on a plane. He'll be staying with your family during the school year. What is your LAL when you meet Aaron?

5. a. You're at swim practice and the coach is going over the schedule for tomorrow night's meet. What is your LAL at swim practice?

    b. You're going home for dinner. Your dad has already left for work and you'll be alone for the evening. What is your LAL when you get home?

6. a. You're leaving school at the end of the day. What is your LAL as you leave school?

    b. Suddenly, you hear the assistant principal call your name. What is your LAL when you hear the assistant principal?

7.   a.   You're watching a horror movie at the theater with your best friend. What is your LAL at the theater?

     b.   You and your best friend are going to meet another friend for pizza. What is your LAL when you meet your friend?

8.   a.   You're running through the mall to catch a bus that's scheduled to leave in two minutes. What is your LAL as you run through the mall?

     b.   A salesclerk stops you as you run and tries to convince you to try a new cologne. What is your LAL when the clerk stops you?

8 Ways to Identify Distractions

Do other students, loud noises, or feeling hungry ever keep you from listening to your teacher? Anything that keeps you from listening is called a *distraction*.

A distraction makes it difficult for you to keep your listening attention level where it should be. This is especially true when you're listening for comprehension.

This handout will help you identify the distractions that make listening difficult.

44   Know what a *distraction* is.

A distraction is anything that pulls your attention away from what you should be listening to. Possible distractions include:

your feelings and emotions		the speaker
hot	upset	her voice
sick	hungry	her gestures
tired	anxious	talking too fast or too slow
angry	excited	talking too loudly or too quietly

things you see or hear
machines
people walking by
insects buzzing around you
noises like whispering, tapping feet, and cracking knuckles
anything you watch or listen to, besides the speaker

45   Ask, "What do I see or hear that's keeping me from listening?"

It's easy to be distracted by people or things around you. A crowd of people, a clock ticking, rain falling, or a pretty spring day can catch your attention and make it hard to listen.

46   Ask, "What is it about the room that's making it hard for me to listen?"

Think about the room's temperature, air circulation, or lighting. It's hard to concentrate in a room with poor light! Is the room comfortable? If it isn't, is there anything you can do to make it more comfortable?

8 Ways to Identify Distractions, *continued*

47 Ask, "Is there anything about the way I'm feeling that's making it hard to be a good listener?"

Your physical condition can sometimes keep you from listening effectively. If you're tired, hungry, sick, or in pain, you'll have a hard time listening to the speaker.

48 Ask, "Are my emotions getting in the way of good listening?"

Sometimes, your emotions can keep you from concentrating. Think about the feelings you're having right now. Are you mad, upset, or nervous about anything? Are your feelings preventing you from paying attention during this activity?

49 Ask, "Is there anything about the speaker that's keeping me from listening?"

Sometimes a person's voice, gestures, or speaking style can keep you from listening. Does the person have a very high or very low pitched voice? Does she use a lot of gestures? Does she use vocabulary that's difficult to understand? Sometimes, a speaker's personal traits can be distracting.

50 Ask, "What is my attitude toward listening?"

What have you told yourself about the current listening situation? Have you already decided, "This class is going to be boring. This speaker doesn't know what she's talking about" or "I already know this stuff"?

Good listeners know that they'll probably learn something from each speaker they listen to. Good listeners also listen with an open mind. They listen to the whole message before they judge the message or the speaker.

51 Realize that you and the people around you might not be bothered by the same things.

Be thoughtful of the people around you. Everyone has different needs when they listen. Everyone's LALs are different.

Perhaps you don't realize that when you tap your pen in class or play your Walkman loudly, the person next to you can't concentrate. On the other hand, you might think a dripping faucet or people whispering are distracting, but the person next to you might not be bothered at all.

Try not to overreact when you're distracted or *you* might become a distraction. The next handout will give you ways to deal with distractions.

What's Distracting You?

Name _____

What are some things that get in the way of your listening? Write examples of the things that distract you. Then, share your answers with your classmates. Can you help each other avoid some distractions?

1. things you see: *friends outside your classroom, cars outside a window, classmates* _____

    passing notes _____

2. things you hear: _____

    _____

3. things about the room: _____

    _____

4. how you feel physically: _____

    _____

5. how you feel emotionally: _____

    _____

6. things about the speaker: _____

    _____

7. things about your attitude toward listening: _____

    _____

That's Distracting!

Underline the possible distractions in each situation below. Use your *8 Ways to Identify Distractions* handout to complete each passage.

1. I went to a play with my stepmom last week. We were late, so I didn't get to eat beforehand. The theater had been built recently and the smell of fresh paint was still pretty strong. But the walls were beautiful! Each wall had a different scene from a famous play painted on it. I couldn't stop looking at them.

   The whole evening would have been enjoyable, except that the air conditioner droned the whole time.

2. Last Thanksgiving, my grandfather told us about his experiences during the war. Grandpa, who's hard of hearing, spoke very loudly as he told us his stories. My mom listened from the kitchen while my dad cleared the table. The rest of us sat in the living room. My two brothers kept poking each other while Grandpa talked.

   I thought Grandpa's stories were interesting and I learned some things I'd never known before. Eventually, my leg fell asleep because I was sitting cross-legged on the floor.

3. Nate went to school yesterday even though he woke up with a sore throat. He wanted to go to school because he was having a test in third period American Literature.

   In first period algebra, his teacher reviewed some concepts from chapter three. Several biology students were conducting a sulfur experiment in the classroom next door to Nate's.

   Toward the end of first period, Nate began to feel hot and wondered if he was getting a fever.

4. The Young Journalists Club had a guest speaker last week. The speaker is an editor of the local newspaper and he spoke about the responsibilities of his job. Every member of the club showed up. It was crowded in the small room.

   The editor knew a lot about the newspaper business, but his voice was hoarse and he coughed a lot. It didn't help that the club met next to the teachers' lounge where delivery men were stacking boxes.

   The meeting was held after school and it lasted an hour longer than most members thought it would. At least the speaker had a lot of interesting things to say.

4 Ways to Get Rid of Distractions

Now you know what distractions are. But do you know what you can do about them? Read this handout to find out.

When you're finished reading this handout, you'll know four ways to get rid of distractions.

52   Identify distractions when you begin listening.

The first step to getting rid of a distraction is deciding what the distractions are. Ask these questions to help you figure out what the distractions are.

What do I see, hear, or feel that's keeping me from listening well?

What is it about the speaker, the room, or the setting that's making it hard for me to concentrate on the speaker's message?

53   Ask yourself if you can get rid of the distraction.

If the distraction is something you see, can you avoid looking at it? If the distraction is something you hear, can you stop the noise or ignore it? If the distraction is the cold temperature in the room, can you put on a sweater or a coat?

You need to decide if you can make a change so you're not distracted any more.

54   Change the environment if you can.

If you can get rid of the distraction, do it!

For example, if people in the hallway become noisy, get up and close the door. If the speaker is talking too softly, raise your hand and ask her to speak louder. If the person sitting next to you is whispering too loudly, move to another seat or politely ask him to whisper more softly. It's up to you to make sure you're able to listen.

55   Set aside the distraction.

If there's nothing you can do about the distraction, try to "set it aside" for the time being.

Try to ignore sounds, smells, and sights that are keeping you from listening. If you have a distracting thought, such as the argument you had earlier with your mom, try not to think about it. Instead, concentrate on your responsibility to listen.

Thinking unrelated thoughts doesn't mean your thoughts are wrong. Tell yourself you'll have time to think about those thoughts later.

Setting distractions aside might be hard at first. But with practice, you'll find that you can do it. Then you'll be able to concentrate on the present listening situation.

5 Ways to Pay Attention

After you get rid of distractions, you're ready to pay attention to the listening situation. But is it always easy to pay attention?

No, it's not, but if you follow the steps below, you'll be a better listener. You'll be able to focus on one thing at a time.

56 Know what you're going to be listening to.

What is the situation or topic of discussion? It's important to know what you're going to be focusing on. This will keep you from being distracted.

57 Know why you're listening.

What is the purpose of your listening? Will you be listening for information, to evaluate, to appreciate, or to understand how someone else feels?

If you know why you're listening, you'll be able to choose your LAL and focus your attention.

58 Identify distractions.

What are you thinking about that will keep you from listening? Are there noises or people distracting you? Is the room too hot or too cold?

Decide what the distractions are before you begin listening.

59 Decide what you can do about the distractions.

Set aside unrelated thoughts, close the door on a noisy hallway, or put on a sweater if you're cold. You're not ready to focus your attention until you've gotten rid of distractions.

60 Relate the topic to your own life.

Try to connect the topic to something you've experienced before. Does the topic remind you of anything? What do you expect to learn? Can you relate the topic to your life so it has more meaning to you?

For example, maybe the speaker is talking about the dangers of driving drunk. You might be able to relate the speaker's information to what you already know about drunk driving.

Relating a topic to your life will make the topic easier to remember.

Coming Into Focus

Name _____

Take some time to practice paying attention. Choose a listening situation, such as a class lecture or a guest speaker, and answer the questions below. See how well the tips you learned for paying attention work for you!

Listening Situation: _____

1. Who am I listening to? _____

2. Why am I listening? _____

3. What is the main topic? _____

4. How does the topic relate to my life? _____

    _____

5. What type of listening will I be doing? _____

6. What thoughts are keeping me from listening well? _____

    _____

7. What else is keeping me from listening? _____

    _____

8. How can I get rid of the distractions? _____

    _____

9. What do I think I'll learn? _____

    _____

Did the focusing attention strategies help you concentrate on the topic? How?

8 Ways to Have a Positive Listening Attitude

As an effective listener, you need to decide if you have a negative or positive attitude toward listening.

If you find that your attitude is negative, you can change to a positive attitude. The eight ways below tell you how.

61   Have a "wait and see" attitude.

Don't judge a speaker, a topic, or a listening situation before you actually begin listening. You won't be an effective listener. Try to keep an open mind and listen to what the speaker has to say before you make any judgments. Listening closely to the whole message will make you a more effective listener.

62   Think of positive outcomes of what you're about to hear.

Set a goal for yourself when you start listening. Tell yourself that you'll feel positive about the listening activity when it's over. If you begin with a positive attitude, you'll probably end with a positive attitude.

Here are some positive outcomes you might think about:

I'll learn about . . . .

I'll be more prepared for my test.

I'll get to know the speaker better.

I'll improve my understanding of . . . .

I'll get more practice in effective listening.

I'll show this person that I care about what she's saying.

63   Don't expect the speaker to entertain you.

Remember, listening is something *you* do. Some speakers aren't as lively as others and some topics aren't as interesting as others. However, you're responsible for your own listening.

If you understand that good listening depends on you, you'll be a better listener.

8 Ways to Have a Positive Listening Attitude, *continued*

64 **Let your posture help your attitude.**

Changing your posture can improve your listening attitude. Sit up straight, face the speaker, and take a quick, deep breath. Often, if you have a good posture, your listening attitude will improve.

65 **Change negative self-talk to positive self-talk.**

For example, if you catch yourself thinking, "This school assembly is boring" or "This guy doesn't know what he's talking about," try to rephrase those negative attitudes into more positive ones. A positive attitude will put you in a better mood to listen. You'll be more open to what the speaker says.

Instead, you might say, "I already know some of this information, but I'll listen anyway because I might learn something" or "I really don't like this speaker, but maybe her topic is interesting."

It's important to remember that even if you don't like a speaker, you might still like what she has to say.

66 **Check your attitude as you listen.**

Always check your attitude before you start to listen. Then, when you've been listening for a while, ask yourself, "What is my listening attitude right now? Do I need to change my attitude?"

Checking your attitude from time to time will remind you to keep an open mind. At the end of the listening situation, you'll be able to make a fair judgment about what you've heard.

67 **Thank the speaker for sharing his ideas.**

If a guest speaker or a classmate has given a speech, tell him he did a good job. If your dad explains how to fix the gears on your bike, tell him you appreciate his help. Sincere appreciation shows a good attitude toward listening. And a good attitude is a sign of a good listener.

68 **Remember that good listening improves your relationships.**

People who listen are more fun to be around than people who talk all the time. Your family, friends, and coworkers will enjoy talking with you if they believe you truly listen to their ideas. Then, they'll be more willing to listen to you when you need someone to talk to.

Go for the Positive!

Name _____

Read the following situations. Change each negative attitude to a positive one.

Then, give at least one positive outcome that might result from listening well.

1. Your best friend asks you to attend a poetry reading by her favorite poet. You first thought is, "I hate poetry!"

   Positive attitude: _____

   _____

   Positive outcome: _____

   _____

2. You've been assigned to listen to a radio talk show. The host, an ex-police officer, is talking about youth gangs. The host has an unusual voice and you disagree with the first two points he makes. You think, "This guy is crazy! What does he know about gangs anyway?"

   Positive attitude: _____

   _____

   Positive outcome: _____

   _____

3. You're at an all-school assembly to hear campaign speeches from candidates for Student Senate. You're thinking, "I really don't care about this stuff!"

   Positive attitude: _____

   _____

   Positive outcome: _____

   _____

Go for the Positive!

Name _____

4. Your volleyball team lost a match today. The coach is beginning one of her lectures. You think, "So what if we lost again! All this talking isn't going to make us a winning team!"

    Positive attitude: _____

    _____

    Positive outcome: _____

    _____

5. During Cultural Awareness Week, a guest speaker from Brazil comes to speak to your class. You're thinking, "Didn't we just finish a unit on Brazil? What's this speaker going to be able to teach us?"

    Positive attitude: _____

    _____

    Positive outcome: _____

    _____

6. You're serving on a committee to plan the Valentine's Day dance. The chairperson suggests you wear a heart costume to sell tickets tomorrow. You say to yourself, "No way! Where did she come up with that idea?"

    Positive attitude: _____

    _____

    Positive outcome: _____

    _____

7. You're watching a film about volcanoes in science class. You think, "This is so boring. Wake me when it's over."

    Positive attitude: _____

    _____

    Positive outcome: _____

    _____

Unit 4: Being an Active Listener

Teacher Tips

Using Mind's Eye, pages 84 to 91
Using Mind's Ear, pages 92 to 95
Remembering Long Messages,
              pages 96 and 97
Listening for What's Important,
              pages 98 to 102

Your students have been learning and practicing some great listening skills. Now they need to learn how to remember what they hear. This unit teaches your students the skills of visualization and re-auditorization, as well as how to listen for verbal cues.

Visualization involves the *mind's eye*. With this strategy, your students will learn to make mental pictures of the information they hear. If someone described his new girlfriend, a student would use his mind's eye to picture the girl in his mind.

Re-auditorization involves the *mind's ear*. Your students can use this strategy to remember short pieces of information. They can silently repeat short messages to themselves to help them remember the messages long enough to write them down.

Typically, people use mind's ear to remember short messages, like phone numbers, addresses, or people they've just met. In the third handout in this unit, your students will learn how to remember longer pieces of information.

In this unit, your students will also learn how to key into certain cue words that prompt them to listen for important information. They'll practice listening for cues and identifying the main idea of passages.

The goal of this unit is to help your students organize and recall information, especially when they're engaged in comprehensive listening. Your students will learn that although they may not be able to change a message, they *can* change their listening approach to a message.

For example, instead of deciding to daydream because a particular science topic is too hard to understand, your students can use the techniques in this unit to make the topic easier to understand.

By learning some strategies that will help them remember information, your students will become more effective listeners.

Handout: 8 Ways to Picture Messages in Your Mind

This handout gives your students some suggestions for using their mind's eye. Discuss the introduction and strategies with your students. Talk about different listening situations when using their mind's eye could be applied. Then, encourage your students to share experiences when they used their mind's eye to help them visualize something.

Activity Sheet: Picture This!

Let your students practice using their mind's eye. Give each student a copy of the activity sheet. Have your students follow the directions you read from page 86 to complete their activity sheets. When they're finished, let your students compare their papers so they can see how different people visualize things.

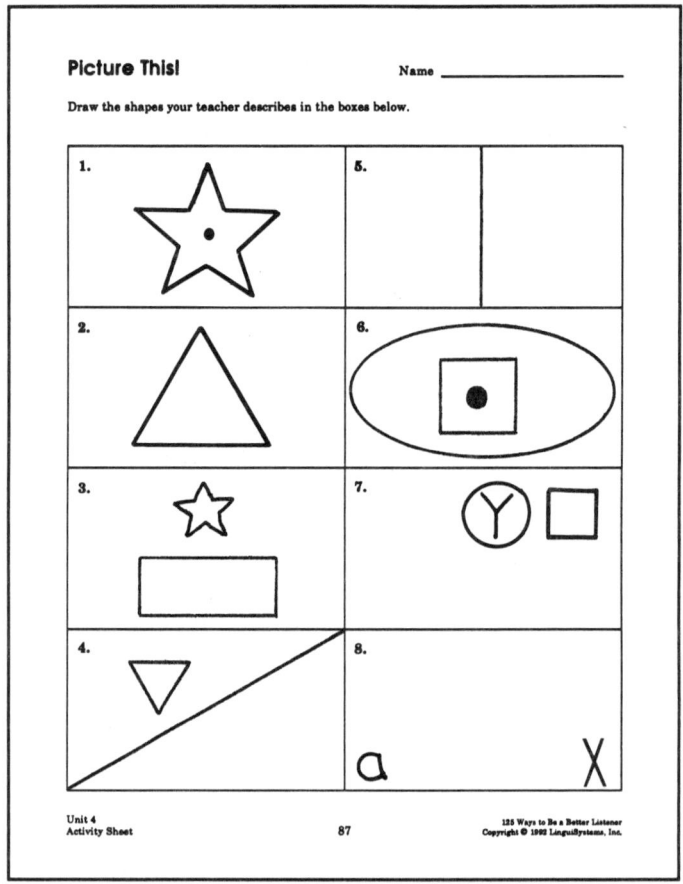

Listening Using Mind's Eye

For this activity, each student will need a sheet of lined paper. Your students will practice visualization as you read increasingly lengthy passages from pages 88 to 91. They'll apply mind's eye strategies as they describe words and sentences, answer questions about paragraphs, and practice giving and following directions.

Discuss your students' responses as they complete each of the four sections. Compare your students' responses and talk about why some items were easier to visualize than others.

Handout: 8 Ways to Remember Short Messages

Read and discuss the introduction of this handout with your students. Your students will use the strategies from this handout to help them recall information. Explain that the mind's ear is most helpful when trying to remember short pieces of information, such as phone numbers, short directions, or sports scores.

Listening Using Mind's Ear

How well can your students use the mind's ear strategies? Here are two activities that will help your students practice their re-auditorization skills. For the first activity, read each sentence on page 94. Then, reread each sentence, omitting the bold words. Have your students tell you which word or words you omitted from each sentence. Ask your students how important the omitted words are to the messages. Do the messages have the same meaning if the words are left out? Finally, discuss the importance of listening closely to messages.

For the second activity, each student will need a sheet of lined paper. Read each sentence on page 95. Encourage your students to repeat the important parts of the message silently. Then, say "Go" and have your students write down the parts of the message they remember. Discuss your students' answers and again decide if the information your students remembered was crucial to the message. Finally, talk about which messages were hard to remember using mind's ear strategies.

Handout: 7 Ways to Remember Long Messages

Your students spend most of their listening time engaging in comprehensive listening. They listen to lectures, directions, and audiotapes throughout the day. These listening situations require them to listen and remember long pieces of information. Discuss this handout of strategies that will help your students tune into and remember long messages.

Handout: 6 Ways to Listen for What's Important

This handout will help your students tune into lengthier pieces of information. Read this handout with your students to explain that cue words and phrases, such as *next, finally, in conclusion,* and the *13 original colonies are . . . ,* let them know what they're about to hear is important. Your students will learn to listen for verbal cues and key words that suggest an important piece of information follows. As your students become more adept at listening for key phrases, they'll become better at listening for signal words.

Activity Sheet: What's Important Here?

For this activity, your students will read five passages. They'll circle the signal words and phrases in each passage Then, they'll determine the main idea of each passage. When your students have completed their activity sheets, help them determine what important information follows each signal word they circled. Finally, discuss the main idea of each passage.

The number at the end of each passage tells how many signal words and phrases your students should look for. Use the directions on the activity sheet as an example of how to complete the activity sheet. Help your students determine what each signal word in the directions means and what the main idea of the directions is. The main idea of the directions is *Students should find the signal words, tell what they mean, and identify the main idea.*

Listening for What's Important

Give your students some real-life practice with listening for verbal cues and identifying main idea. Read some passages from your students' textbooks aloud. Or, bring in a newspaper and read some headlines and articles to your students. Explain that headlines are often mini-summaries of the articles.

Have your students listen for the signal words in each article. Then, have your students determine the main idea of each article.

Remember to read slowly enough for your students to practice their skills, increasing your speed as your students become more adept.

What's Important Here?　　Name _____

Use tips 95 and 96 from your handout *6 Ways to Listen for What's Important* to complete these activity sheets.

First read each passage. Then reread the passage and circle the signal words as you read. The number after each passage tells you how many signal words are in that passage. Finally write the main idea of each passage. The main idea can usually be stated in a single sentence. (4)

1. The city council wants to recycle the trash that's piling up at the local landfill. Recycling will have two effects. First, recycling will save important landfill space. Plus, fewer resources will be needed to make new products.

   The city's recycling center will accept newspapers and aluminum cans. In addition, the center will take glass jars, flattened cardboard boxes, and plastic jugs. (4)

   What is the main idea of this passage? *The city's new recycling center will be good for the environment.*

2. You need to remember five things when you set up an aquarium. First, rinse the tank and gravel with plain tap water. Never use soap or detergent.

   Second, pour the gravel in the tank. Third, pour water slowly into the tank so you don't disturb the gravel. Fill the tank only half way.

   Fourth, add plants and the rest of the water.

   Finally, attach the air pump and water filter and let them run for at least a week before you add the fish. (6)

   What is the main idea of this passage? *There are five important steps to follow for setting up an aquarium.*

What's Important Here?　　Name _____

3. The Great Lakes are located between the United States and Canada. The five lakes are Lake Superior, Lake Michigan, Lake Huron, Lake Erie, and Lake Ontario. Only one of the lakes, Lake Michigan, is completely in the United States. There are three canals that help ships travel between the lakes. The canals are the Welland Canal, the Soo Canal, and the Saint Lawrence Seaway. The canals are extremely important to world trade. Ships carry steel, wheat, coal, ore, and cars to other parts of the world. (4)

   What is the main idea of this passage? *The Great Lakes and the canals that connect them are important to world trade.*

4. The Great Wall of China is truly a wondrous site. The wall is the largest wall ever built. It's more than 1500 miles long. In addition to its length, the wall is also the highest ever built. It measures 25 feet high in some places. Towers along the wall are from 35 to 40 feet high. The wall follows a remarkable path. It goes over mountains and through valleys in a course that's the distance from New York City to Omaha, Nebraska. (5)

   What is the main idea of this passage? *The Great Wall of China is remarkable for many reasons.*

5. Today we'll talk about our attitudes toward balanced diets. Many of us understand the value of a balanced diet, but few of us eat a balanced diet. Why is this, you might ask. Simply, the issue is convenience. We're more interested in eating food that's easy to prepare than in food that's good for us. We're so busy, we grab whatever is available.

   Of equal importance is the desire to avoid cooking. If we do cook, it's often with convenience foods that take little time to prepare. But it's possible to make meals that are good for you and easy to make. Quick, nutritious recipes will be the focus of our class today. (5)

   What is the main idea of this passage? *It's important and easy to follow a balanced diet.*

6. Three people in my family are getting ready for the Harvest Festival. My sister has been baking corn cakes that are sweetened with honey. My father not only carved and painted a dancer's mask but he also wrote a history of the festival.

   Now that I'm old enough to participate in the thanksgiving dance, I've been practicing every evening. In addition to these preparations, we're making costumes for the opening parade. (3)

   What is the main idea of this passage? *My family is busy preparing for the Harvest Festival.*

Additional Activities

★ Read the following descriptions to your students. Next, discuss the different images each student visualized as he listened. Finally, have students take turns reading descriptions from their textbooks as other students visualize what's being read.

1. It has a stout body that's covered with coarse hair. Its nose is black and pointed, and its ears are small. It has a black patch around each eye. There's a ring of white fur around the black patch. The tail is bushy. *raccoon*

2. It has been sitting next to the barn for years. It's faded from being in the sun too long. It has brown rust all over its metal body. Grandpa told me about the day when he first drove her home. It's hard to believe the old tires were once new. *old, abandoned car or farm equipment*

3. Everyone is starting to arrive. The band hasn't started playing yet, but people are walking around, talking with each other. They think the decorations look great. The women are wearing formal dresses and the men have tuxedos or formal suits on. *dance or reception*

★ Write the following images on cards. Then, let each student choose a card and describe the image for the rest of the class. Or, read each card to your students and have each student write what comes to mind when he hears each item. Then, let your students share their answers to compare how different people view the same things.

raging fire	rock concert
natural disaster	party
vacation	city street
national monument	severe weather

★ Play *Telephone*! Whisper a message in one student's ear. Have that student repeat what he heard to another student. Continue until all students have heard the message. Then, have the last student say the message that he heard out loud. Finally, discuss why it can be difficult to keep messages accurate.

Or, divide your class into two groups. Give both groups the same message. Have each group play *Telephone*. Ask the last student in each group to write the message on a piece of paper. Then, see whose message is closest to the original one.

8 Ways to Picture Messages in Your Mind

If someone told you about a great movie he'd seen, would you be able to picture the characters and scenery in your mind? If the Fall Dance Committee were talking about decorating the gym, could you picture what the gym would look like the night of the dance?

When you picture things in your head, you're using your *mind's eye*. Good listeners use their mind's eye throughout their lives. They try to picture information as they hear it. Using your mind's eye to picture information can help you remember the information.

Read the tips below to learn how to use your mind's eye.

69   Try to see what you hear.

When you listen to directions or to a description, imagine a picture in your mind. For example, if your teacher is describing the process of evaporation, imagine water turning into a gas and rising into the air.

Most people remember what they *see* longer than they remember what they *hear*. So try to see information as you hear it.

70   Close your eyes.

Some information is harder to imagine than other information. It might help to close your eyes while you use your mind's eye. If your math teacher says you're daydreaming, tell him you're learning. Tell him you're imagining the area of a triangle as he explains it to the class!

71   Use all your senses when you make pictures in your mind.

Add sounds, smells, and colors to your picture.

If a classmate is reporting about a Civil War battle, imagine the sound of muskets, the smell of gunpowder, and the colors of the soldiers' uniforms. You'll be surprised at how much information you remember. Plus, your pictures will make the report more interesting to listen to.

72   Add emotions and feelings to your pictures.

Instead of just listening to a TV program, try to imagine how a character is feeling. Ask yourself how you would feel if you were that character. If you can relate emotionally to what you hear, the message will be more meaningful.

8 Ways to Picture Messages in Your Mind, *continued*

73   Think of words to go with your pictures.

When you a hear a new idea for the first time, picture the written word in your mind. Then, add a scene to go along with the word.

For example, say a speaker is telling about the parts of a car engine. Try to see the words *engine*, *battery*, and *oil filter* in your mind.   Then, picture a car engine as the speaker talks about it.

74   Be creative.

The more unusual your pictures are, the more likely you'll remember the information you're listening to. And remember, your mind's eye pictures will probably be very different from everyone else's pictures. That's because you have a one-of-a-kind imagination!

75   Make the action words you hear come alive.

Listen as your teacher talks about herds of deer running across a field. Try to picture the animals as they gracefully leap across the field. Listen as your friend describes how he raced through the street to catch a bus. Try to picture your friend dodging traffic as he runs toward the departing bus.

If you can picture the action in a message, the message will become more interesting. And interesting messages are often easy to remember.

76   Draw a picture of the new idea.

The best follow-up to picturing information in your mind is to draw an actual picture of it. Your drawn pictures don't have to be complex. A symbol is a good example of a picture.

Think of the first time you heard the words *appreciative listening*. What's a good way to remember what *appreciative listening* means? First, you could write the words *appreciative listening* on a piece of paper. Then, you could draw a musical note or instrument to help you remember that *appreciative listening* means *listening for enjoyment*.

Picture This!

Use your mind's eye to fill in the boxes on your activity sheets. Listen to the directions I give. Picture the shapes I describe before you draw them in the boxes. (Periodically remind your students to picture the shapes before they draw them.)

1. Draw a triangle in the center of box 2.

2. Draw a vertical line to divide box 5 exactly in half.

3. Draw a square in the upper right-hand corner of box 7. (pause) Draw a circle with the capital letter Y in it next to the square.

4. Draw a dot inside a star in the center of box 1.

5. Draw a capital X in the lower right-hand corner and a small A in the lower left-hand corner of box 8.

6. In box 4, draw a diagonal line from the upper right-hand corner to the lower left-hand corner. (pause) Draw an upside-down triangle on the left-hand side of the line you drew.

7. Draw a horizontal rectangle with a star above it in the center of box 3.

8. Draw a horizontal oval that completely fills the space in box 6. (pause) Draw a circle inside a square in the center of the oval. (pause) Color in the smallest shape in box 6.

Picture This!

Name _____

Draw the shapes your teacher describes in the boxes below.

1.	**5.**
2.	**6.**
3.	**7.**
4.	**8.**

Listening Using Mind's Eye

A. Words

Number your paper from one to ten. I'm going to read some words to you. Try to get a picture in your mind of each word I read.

After you form a picture, write two words that will help you remember the picture. Later, you'll see if the two words you wrote help you remember the word I give you. Let's do the first word together. (Have your students save their responses to use later.)

1. party
2. building
3. race
4. Alaska
5. test

6. muscle
7. discover
8. measure
9. silent
10. hibernate

B. Sentences

(Your students will give oral responses for this section. Pause after each item for your students to describe the pictures they see with their mind's eye.) I'm going to read some sentences to you. After each sentence, I'll ask some of you to describe the pictures you formed in your minds.

Remember, everyone will form a slightly different picture. It'll be interesting to see how different people pictured each sentence!

1. This place is warm and sunny.
2. We're having an all-school assembly this afternoon.
3. The teacher didn't think the joke was funny.
4. The center of a bone is filled with marrow.
5. There's a fire!
6. My younger brother put three cups of dishwashing liquid in the dishwater.
7. I missed my bus.
8. The baby won't stop crying.
9. The mountain climbers struggled in the cold wind to reach the next foothold.
10. Don't judge a book by its cover.

Listening Using Mind's Eye

C. Paragraphs

Let's try something a little different. Number your papers from one to nine. This time, I'll read some paragraphs while you listen. As I read, use your mind's eye to get a picture of the information I give. After I read each paragraph, I'll ask you some questions. Write your answers to the questions on your papers.

(After your students answer the questions to each passage, talk about the pictures they formed as they listened to you read. Periodically remind your students to use their mind's eye to visualize the information you read.)

1. My new niece is so cute! She's only five weeks old, and she weighs almost nine pounds. She eats and sleeps a lot. Her tiny clothes look adorable on her. Her little hands feel so strong when she grabs my finger.

   How old is the speaker's niece? *five weeks*
   Can the baby grab things? *yes*

2. One way to remember what you hear or read is to write an outline. An outline helps you organize information into categories. Outlines make good study guides, too.

   What is the paragraph I just read about? *an outline*
   What can you use an outline for? *to organize information, to study*

3. Three sports invented by Americans include baseball, football, and basketball. Baseball is based on an old English game called *Rounders*. Football is based on rugby, another English sport. Basketball isn't based on any other sport. It started in Massachusetts in the late 1800s.

   What American game did Rounders become? *baseball*
   Which sport started in America? *basketball*

4. Land and water make up the surface of the earth. Large land masses are called continents. There are seven continents on earth.

   What are large land masses called? *continents*
   How many continents are there? *seven*

5. All living things are made up of cells. Every cell has a nucleus. The nucleus, located in the center of the cell, controls the cell's activities.

   Where is the nucleus of a cell located? *in the center of the cell*

Listening Using Mind's Eye

6. Turtles, crocodiles, and lizards are reptiles. Reptiles have skin made of hard scales. Many reptiles live in water, but they need oxygen to breathe, so they have to come to the surface often. Reptiles use their claws to dig and climb.

   Is the paragraph about turtles or reptiles? *reptiles*
   Do reptiles have smooth or rough skin? *rough*
   Name one reptile. *Answers will vary.*

7. The plant life that grows in different parts of the world is called *vegetation*. Vegetation can be found in a variety of regions, including the desert, the forest, and the tundra. The tundra, which is located in polar regions, is a type of plain. Small plants and mosses grow in the tundra.

   Which region includes the most trees? *forest*
   Is the tundra hot or cold? *cold*

8. Lonnie lives with his dad and grandmother in an apartment downtown. Yesterday morning, Lonnie went with his dad's girlfriend, Jenna, to report that Jenna's car had been broken into. The police officer told Jenna that her car stereo probably wouldn't be found. Lonnie said Jenna filed a report with the police officer. Later that afternoon, Jenna called her insurance agent.

   Where does Lonnie live? *in an apartment, downtown*
   What was stolen from Jenna's car? *a stereo, radio*
   Who did Jenna talk to in the afternoon? *her insurance agent*

9. In the western part of North America is a chain of mountains called the Rocky Mountains. These mountains are higher than any mountains in the eastern United States. Even though the Rockies are 130 million years old, they're considered a young mountain chain.

   The peaks of the Rockies form part of the Great Divide, which separates the rivers flowing west to the Pacific Ocean from rivers flowing east to the Atlantic Ocean.

   Are there mountains in the eastern United States? *yes*
   What parts of the Rockies form the Great Divide? *the peaks*
   True or false? Rivers that flow west flow to the Atlantic Ocean. *false*
   Would you travel east or west from Ohio to get to the Rocky Mountains? *west*

(At this point, have your students take out their responses to *Section A, Words*. Ask your students to use their responses to help them remember the original words you gave them. Have your students read their responses to themselves and write the original words next to them. Discuss how using their mind's eye helped your students remember the words.)

Listening Using Mind's Eye

D. Directions

(Write each sentence below on an index card. Play a direction-following game by dividing your class into two teams. Have each student choose a card and give directions to the teams. Encourage your students to have fun with their directions! They might like to give the most round-about way to get to their locations. The team that guesses the target location first gets two points. Play until all the cards have been chosen.)

1. Give directions to a rest room.
2. Give directions to the nurse's office.
3. Give directions to the teachers' lounge.
4. Give directions to the parking lot.
5. Give directions to the gymnasium.
6. Give directions to a Resource Center.
7. Give directions to the cafeteria.
8. Give directions to the main office.
9. Give directions to the teacher's room.
10. Give directions to the science lab.
11. Give directions to the main lobby.
12. Give directions to the football field.
13. Give directions to the music room.
14. Give directions to the custodian's office.
15. Give directions to the place of your choice.
16. Give directions to the place of your choice.

Here's a game to practice using your mind's eye. Everyone will choose a card. Then, each of you will tell the two teams how to get from the room you're in to the location that's written on your card. The team that guesses the location first gets two points. Remember, don't say the location – just tell how to get there.

If you're giving directions, picture the route in your mind. If you're listening to the directions, use your mind's eye to picture where the directions are telling you to go.

8 Ways to Remember Short Messages

How do you remember someone's phone number when she gives it to you? When you're first introduced to someone, how do you remember his name?

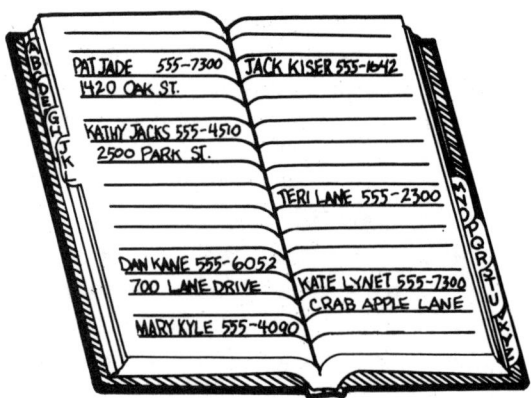

If you want to remember a short message such as a phone number, a birth date, or an address, repeat it to yourself so you hear it in your mind.

Repeating a short message helps you remember the message until you can write it down. Whenever you repeat information to yourself, you're using a very good listening strategy. You're using the strategy known as *mind's ear*.

Read the tips below to help you improve your mind's ear.

77   Repeat words, phrases, and short sentences to yourself.

When you repeat something, you're actually hearing it again. When you hear something more than once, you're likely to remember it longer.

78   Use your mind's ear to remember people's names.

It's not always easy to remember the names of people you've just met. To help you remember someone's name, repeat it when you're first introduced. Say, "It's nice to meet you, Mr. Campbell" or "Hi, Shawnette, how are you?"

79   Use your mind's ear to remember main ideas.

Use your mind's ear to repeat the main points of a lecture or a conversation. If you repeat the main ideas, you'll remember the information the speaker wants you to know.

80   Use your mind's ear to remember short messages.

Use your mind's ear to remember short pieces of information long enough to write them down. The next handout will give you tips for remembering longer messages.

8 Ways to Remember Short Messages, *continued*

81   Write the message down as soon as possible.

Remember, your mind's ear helps you remember important information for a short time. But if you want to remember the information longer, write it down. Then, use your written notes later to help you remember the information.

82   Use your mind's ear to "think along" with the speaker.

During a lecture or a casual conversation, silently repeat the speaker's ideas. This will help you concentrate and think about the points the speaker is trying to make.

83   Use your mind's eye and your mind's ear at the same time.

Using both strategies will really improve your memory! When you hear a phone number for the first time, picture the number in your mind (mind's eye), repeat the number to yourself (mind's ear), then write the number down as soon as possible.

If you follow this tip, it's as if someone had told you her phone number three times instead of just once!

84   Decide if the information you just heard makes sense.

Some information is confusing. For example, your boss might say, "I have meetings at 2:00 and 5:30, but I'll be back when it's over." You don't know if your boss will be back after the 2:00 meeting or after the 5:30 meeting. Your boss' information is confusing.

Or a friend might say, "I can't decide if I want to go to the dance with Kyle or Gavin. Do you think I should ask him?" How can you answer your friend's question? You don't know if she's talking about Kyle or about Gavin. Her question is confusing.

If you're not sure you understand a message you hear, *ask questions*!

Listening Using Mind's Ear

Listen to the sentences I read. I'll read each sentence twice. The first time I read the sentence, use your mind's ear to repeat it to yourself. The second time I read the sentence, I'm going to leave out one or more words. Use your mind's ear to decide which word or words I left out.

Then, we'll discuss whether the meaning of the sentence changes when I leave some words out. We'll also talk about the importance of listening carefully to messages so you hear the information you need.

1. Don't wear **dark**-colored clothing for your class picture.

2. Turn off the light, **please**. You're wasting electricity.

3. There will be a Single Parents meeting **this Saturday** at noon.

4. For the semester exam, be sure to study chapters 12, **16**, 26, and 28.

5. Mr. Walters spoke to the **sophomore** class about advertising careers.

6. Alligators and flamingos live in **Florida and** Georgia.

7. Yesterday, we placed second in the **mural-painting** competition.

8. Please pick the kids up **from day care at 3:15** this afternoon.

9. My manager asked me **to tell Pauline** to clean the soda pop machine.

10. **After she has surgery,** Mrs. Lee will take medication for her heart condition.

11. Our class will take a field trip to the mall **to learn about comparison shopping**.

12. If **you fail to report to the office after** you're absent, you'll receive a three-day detention.

13. Ray**'s brother** was voted **both class clown and** most likely to succeed.

14. The youth group had a car wash to raise money for **sports equipment and art supplies at** the youth center.

15. Last summer, volunteers **from the Big Brothers/Big Sisters program** took us to **a history museum and to** a baseball game.

Listening Using Mind's Ear

Listen to the messages I read. Use your mind's ear to repeat the most important information in each message. Then when I say go, write down the important part of the message. Remember, you don't need to repeat the whole message – just the most important part. Here's an example.

Ex. You want to know when Anne's birthday is. It's September 19. Go.

What's the most important information in that message? That's right. The date of Anne's birthday is important. You should have written *Anne's birthday – September 19.* (Encourage your students to use simple abbreviations they know, such as *b-day* and *9/19.* Challenge your students to hold each message in their memories by waiting varying lengths of time before you say, "Go.")

1. An oil change for my car will cost twenty-four dollars and ninety-five cents. Go.
    oil change – $24.95

2. Junior varsity swim practice has been changed from 3:15 to 3:45. Go. *JV swim 3:45*

3. Buses 88, 91, and 243 will be 10 minutes late. Go. *88, 91, 243 – 10 minutes late*

4. Read pages 98 through 103 and pages 107 through 109. Go. *98 – 103, 107 – 109*

5. Take a half teaspoon of this prescription every three hours, but not on an empty stomach. Go. *1/2 tsp / 3 hrs, eat first*

6. For more information about the American Cancer Federation, call 1-800-555-2747. Go. *ACF, 1-800- 555-2747*

7. At quarter to 11 this morning, it was 52 degrees outside. Go. *10:45, 52°*

8. The movie *Star Seekers* is showing at 1:30, 3:45, 6:00, and 8:15. Go.
    Star Seekers – 1:30, 3:45, 6:00, 8:15

9. If you drop your film off by 2:00, you can pick it up the next day. Go.
    2:00 today, pick up tomorrow

10. On your first day of work, ask to speak with Georgia Mast. Go. *see Georgia Mast*

11. The suspect was driving a dark blue car with a smashed front fender. The license plate read MCM223. Go. *dk. blue, smashed fender, MCM223*

12. To get to the video arcade, take 58th Street to Orange Avenue. Go left on Orange Avenue. Then take a right on Pine Street. The arcade will be on your left. Go.
    58th Street, l. on Orange, r. on Pine

13. If the month you were born in is an even number, line up behind Danielle. If the month you were born in is an odd number, line up behind Sean. Go. *Answers will vary, depending on birth dates.*

7 Ways to Remember Long Messages

As a good listener, you'll use your mind's ear to remember short messages. But you need different listening strategies to remember longer messages. Use the tips below to help you remember long messages.

85   **Know the topic of the message.**

Listen for the speaker to state the topic. Often your teachers will tell you what you'll be working on at the beginning of class. Or your boss will tell you what jobs he wants you to finish by the end of the day. The first step to remembering long messages is knowing what the message is about!

86   **See if the speaker writes what he says.**

Any information a speaker says *and* writes at the same time is probably important. For example, if your teacher is lecturing, watch for him to write important dates or words on the chalkboard or on an overhead.

87   **Use your mind's eye.**

Picture the speaker's message in your mind. If your mom is telling you about her new job, try to picture your mom in her workplace. If your driver's ed teacher is telling you what to do if your car slides on ice, picture yourself turning the steering wheel to straighten the car.

Remember, making pictures in your mind can be a powerful memory tool.

88   **Use your mind's ear.**

Repeat the speaker's message when you hear it. You already know that repeating information helps you remember short messages. Now you know that repeating information helps you remember long messages, too.

89   **Don't repeat the message word for word.**

Yes it's smart to repeat a message to yourself. But don't get carried away. Instead, focus only on the main points of the message.

Say a friend is telling you about a party he wants you to go to. Maybe he's telling you the people who will be at the party, what he plans to wear, and where the party is. His whole message about the party might be interesting, but the main point of the message is where the party is.

Don't repeat the message word for word.
Don't repeat the message word for word.
Don't repeat the message word for word.

7 Ways to Remember Long Messages, *continued*

90   **Take notes.**

Get your hands moving! The more involved you are with the listening process, the better you'll be able to remember information. Write down main ideas and points you feel are most important.

Don't worry about getting every word down on paper. Use most of your energy to listen, not to write.

91   **Relate the new information to information you already know.**

Decide how the new information is similar to information you've learned in the past. For example, say you're learning to play soccer and you already know how to play football. Your knowledge of football will help you learn the new sport.

6 Ways to Listen for What's Important

The last handout gave you some tips for remembering long messages. But do you know how to *listen* for the important information in a long message? Do you know how to tell if information you hear is worth remembering?

Actually, speakers give lots of hints as they speak. These hints tell you that what you're about to hear is important. If you learn to listen to these hints, you won't miss important information.

Read this handout for some simple ways to listen for important information.

92   Listen for the main idea.

Most speakers place their main ideas in only a few places. You'll often hear the main idea:

    a. in the title of a speech or presentation.
    b. soon after the speaker begins to talk.
    c. at the end of a speech.

Listen closely to the beginning and end of a speech so you won't miss the main idea.

93   Listen to the speaker's voice.

Often a speaker will stress an important point. If you listen closely to the speaker, you'll notice her voice becomes louder and slower when she makes an important point. Listen closely to a speaker's voice. Her voice could be telling you to listen up!

94   Listen for the speaker to repeat herself.

Pay close attention to pieces of information that a speaker repeats. If someone says an idea more than once, the idea is probably important.

95   Listen for signal words.

Many speakers use certain signal words to let you know that what they're about to say is important. These words are clues that you should listen very closely. Signal words tell you a variety of information.

Some signal words tell you how many points the speaker is going to make. Other signal words let you know that the speaker is about to change topics.

You'll find examples of signal words and the kind of information they signal on page 99.

6 Ways to Listen for What's Important, *continued*

Number of Points

There are nine planets.
The three Scandinavian countries are . . .
The following six students should stay after class.

Order of Steps

First, . . . second, . . . last, . . .
Then, . . . next, . . . finally, . . .

Main Idea

I want you to understand one thing . . .
Today we're going to talk about . . .
Simply, the issue is . . .
In conclusion, I want you to remember . . .
To summarize . . .
Most important, . . .

Supporting Ideas

Not only _____, but also . . .
Next in importance is . . .
In addition to this . . .
A second cause is . . .
Another reason . . .

Changing Topics

On the other hand, . . .
Turning to something new, . . .

Adjectives and Describing Words

awful	cleanest
beautiful	remarkable
awesome	horrible
terrible	greatest

6 Ways to Listen for What's Important, *continued*

96   Listen for other important words.

Listen for numbers.   Numbers tell you how many pages to read, how many problems to do, and how many pages long a report should be.

You should also listen carefully to your teacher's directions.   Important words in directions tell you what to do.

Some important words include:

circle	read
draw	listen
underline	fill in
choose	state
write	remember

97   Ask yourself questions.

Asking yourself questions as you listen is a good way to focus your listening.   You might ask, "What's the most important thing this speaker wants me to remember?   Do I agree with everything the speaker has said?" and "Did I understand the last point the speaker made?"

If you can't answer your own questions, ask the speaker to explain himself again.

What's Important Here?

Name _____

Use tips 95 and 96 from your handout *6 Ways to Listen for What's Important* to complete these activity sheets.

First, read each passage. Then, reread the passage and circle the signal words as you read. The number after each passage tells you how many signal words are in that passage. Finally, write the main idea of each passage. The main idea can usually be stated in a single sentence. (4)

1. The city council wants to recycle the trash that's piling up at the local landfill. Recycling will have two effects. First, recycling will save important landfill space. Plus, fewer resources will be needed to make new products.

    The city's recycling center will accept newspapers and aluminum cans. In addition, the center will take glass jars, flattened cardboard boxes, and plastic jugs. (4)

    What is the main idea of this passage? _____

    _____

2. You need to remember five things when you set up an aquarium. First, rinse the tank and gravel with plain tap water. Never use soap or detergent.

    Second, pour the gravel in the tank. Third, pour water slowly into the tank so you don't disturb the gravel. Fill the tank only halfway.

    Fourth, add plants and the rest of the water.

    Finally, attach the air pump and water filter and let them run for at least a week before you add the fish. (6)

    What is the main idea of this passage? _____

    _____

What's Important Here?

3. The Great Lakes are located between the United States and Canada. The five lakes are Lake Superior, Lake Michigan, Lake Huron, Lake Erie, and Lake Ontario. Only one of the lakes, Lake Michigan, is completely in the United States. There are three canals that help ships travel between the lakes. The canals are the Welland Canal, the Soo Canal, and the Saint Lawrence Seaway. The canals are extremely important to world trade. Ships carry steel, wheat, coal, ore, and cars to other parts of the world. (4)

What is the main idea of this passage? _____

_____

4. The Great Wall of China is truly a wondrous site. The wall is the largest wall ever built. It's more than 1500 miles long. In addition to its length, the wall is also the highest ever built. It measures 25 feet high in some places. Towers along the wall are from 35 to 40 feet high. The wall follows a remarkable path. It goes over mountains and through valleys in a course that's the distance from New York City to Omaha, Nebraska. (5)

What is the main idea of this passage? _____

_____

5. Today we'll talk about our attitudes toward balanced diets. Many of us understand the value of a balanced diet, but few of us eat a balanced diet. Why is this, you might ask. Simply, the issue is convenience. We're more interested in eating food that's easy to prepare than in food that's good for us. We're so busy, we grab whatever is available.

Of equal importance is the desire to avoid cooking. If we do cook, it's often with convenience foods that take little time to prepare. But, it's possible to make meals that are good for you and easy to make. Quick, nutritious recipes will be the focus of our class today. (5)

What is the main idea of this passage? _____

_____

6. Three people in my family are getting ready for the Harvest Festival. My sister has been baking corn cakes that are sweetened with honey. My father not only carved and painted a dancer's mask, but he also wrote a history of the festival.

Now that I'm old enough to participate in the thanksgiving dance, I've been practicing every evening. In addition to these preparations, we're making costumes for the opening parade. (3)

What is the main idea of this passage? _____

_____

Unit 5: Responding to the Message

Teacher Tips

> Giving Feedback, pages 108 to 117
> Asking Questions, pages 118 to 121

Your students have been learning that listening is an active process. They've learned that they're responsible for their own listening and for understanding the message. In this unit, your students will learn that responding to a speaker can help their understanding of a message.

The unit focuses on the listener's responsibility for giving feedback and for asking questions during the communication process. Begin the unit by discussing feedback with your students. Explain that feedback is simply a response to a message. Put the following chart on the chalkboard.

Verbal	Nonverbal
saying "uh-huh"	nodding
asking questions	looking confused
repeating the message	daydreaming
laughing	making eye contact

Discuss the differences between verbal and nonverbal feedback with your students. Keep the chart on the chalkboard for your students to refer to throughout the unit.

After your students understand what feedback is, give them the handouts and activity sheets. Explain that giving feedback and asking questions help listeners and speakers communicate better. In the classroom, teachers want to know that your students understand their lectures. Outside of school, friends and employers need to know that your students are truly listening to and understanding their messages.

This unit will teach your students that giving effective feedback and asking appropriate questions makes them better listeners.

Handout: 5 Ways to Give Verbal Feedback

This handout gives your students some practical hints about verbal feedback during conversation. Discuss the introduction with your students. Then, talk about the strategies so your students will know that verbal feedback is necessary for good communication.

Handout: 5 Ways to Improve Your Verbal Feedback

This handout further explains verbal feedback. It will help your students know what to say when they give verbal feedback. It also helps them understand how and when verbal feedback is most effective.

Handout: 9 Ways to Give Nonverbal Feedback

Eye contact, facial expression, vocal inflection, and posture are forms of nonverbal feedback. This handout explains why nonverbal feedback is so powerful. Use this handout to talk about when nonverbal feedback would be most appropriate during your students' daily activities.

Activity Sheet: Give Me Some Feedback!

Your students will have fun as they practice giving feedback to convey a variety of emotions. First, give each student a copy of the *Give Me Some Feedback!* activity sheet to complete. Encourage your students to refer to the chart you put on the chalkboard (see page 103, Teacher Tips) to help them remember types of feedback.

Then, ask volunteers to role-play situations illustrating the emotions on the activity sheet. For example, Lisa might tell Karl that she won the election for class president. Have Karl give Lisa feedback that shows he's happy about Lisa's news.

Give Me Some Feedback!   Name _____

Your emotions often determine the feedback you give in a certain situation. Read the emotions below and think about times you've felt each one. Then, write the kinds of verbal and nonverbal feedback you might give to show your feelings. The first one is done for you as an example.

Emotion	Verbal	Nonverbal
1. happy	*"I feel great today!"*	*smile, give thumbs-up sign*
2. angry	*Answers will vary.*	
3. bored		
4. excited		
5. embarrassed		
6. worried		
7. proud		
8. confused		

Unit 5
Activity Sheet   115   125 Ways to Be a Better Listener
Copyright © 1992 LinguiSystems, Inc.

Activity Sheet: Mixed Messages

This activity sheet will help your students understand how the most effective kinds of verbal and nonverbal feedback complement each other. Your students will read situations in which the nonverbal feedback contradicts the verbal feedback to create a mixed message. Ask your students to tell why the two kinds of feedback contradict one another.

Then, have your students discuss ways to change either the verbal or the nonverbal response so that the responses are complementary. Finally, let your students tell about their personal experiences with "mixed messages."

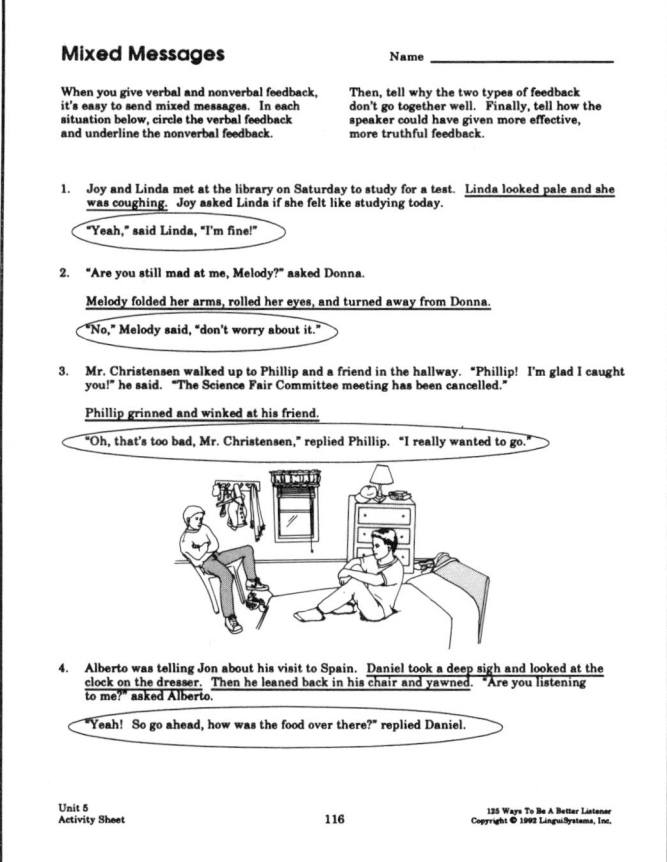

Mixed Messages　　　　Name _____

When you give verbal and nonverbal feedback, it's easy to send mixed messages. In each situation below, circle the verbal feedback and underline the nonverbal feedback.

Then, tell why the two types of feedback don't go together well. Finally, tell how the speaker could have given more effective, more truthful feedback.

1. Joy and Linda met at the library on Saturday to study for a test. Linda looked pale and she was coughing. Joy asked Linda if she felt like studying today.

   "Yeah," said Linda, "I'm fine!"

2. "Are you still mad at me, Melody?" asked Donna.

   Melody folded her arms, rolled her eyes, and turned away from Donna.

   "No," Melody said, "don't worry about it."

3. Mr. Christensen walked up to Phillip and a friend in the hallway. "Phillip! I'm glad I caught you!" he said. "The Science Fair Committee meeting has been cancelled."

   Phillip grinned and winked at his friend.

   "Oh, that's too bad, Mr. Christensen," replied Phillip. "I really wanted to go."

4. Alberto was telling Jon about his visit to Spain. Daniel took a deep sigh and looked at the clock on the dresser. Then he leaned back in his chair and yawned. "Are you listening to me?" asked Alberto.

   "Yeah! So go ahead, how was the food over there?" replied Daniel.

Unit 5
Activity Sheet　　116　　125 Ways To Be A Better Listener Copyright © 1992 LinguiSystems, Inc.

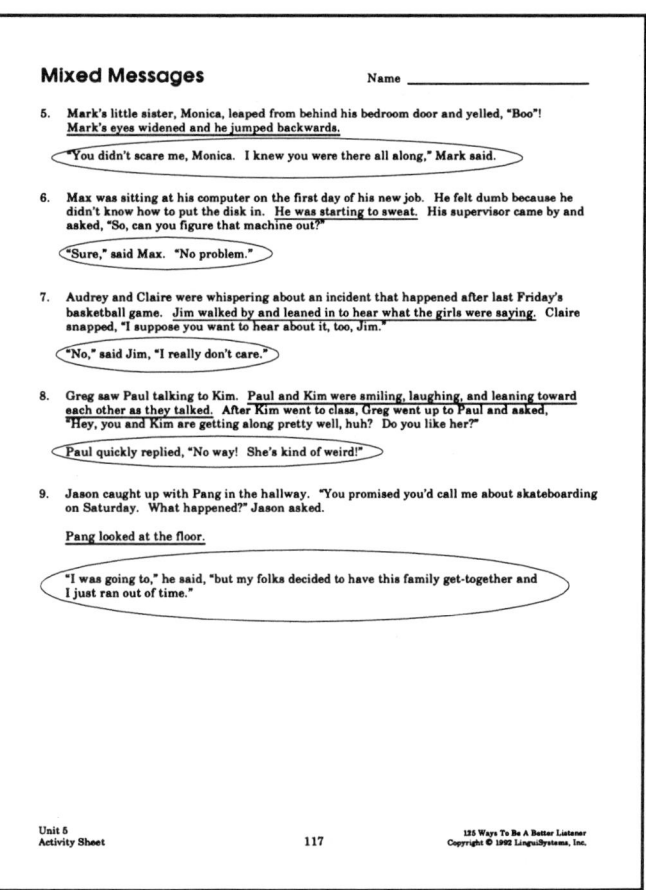

Mixed Messages　　　　Name _____

5. Mark's little sister, Monica, leaped from behind his bedroom door and yelled, "Boo"! Mark's eyes widened and he jumped backwards.

   "You didn't scare me, Monica. I knew you were there all along," Mark said.

6. Max was sitting at his computer on the first day of his new job. He felt dumb because he didn't know how to put the disk in. He was starting to sweat. His supervisor came by and asked, "So, can you figure that machine out?"

   "Sure," said Max. "No problem."

7. Audrey and Claire were whispering about an incident that happened after last Friday's basketball game. Jim walked by and leaned in to hear what the girls were saying. Claire snapped, "I suppose you want to hear about it, too, Jim."

   "No," said Jim, "I really don't care."

8. Greg saw Paul talking to Kim. Paul and Kim were smiling, laughing, and leaning toward each other as they talked. After Kim went to class, Greg went up to Paul and asked, "Hey, you and Kim are getting along pretty well, huh? Do you like her?"

   Paul quickly replied, "No way! She's kind of weird!"

9. Jason caught up with Pang in the hallway. "You promised you'd call me about skateboarding on Saturday. What happened?" Jason asked.

   Pang looked at the floor.

   "I was going to," he said, "but my folks decided to have this family get-together and I just ran out of time."

Unit 5
Activity Sheet　　117　　125 Ways To Be A Better Listener Copyright © 1992 LinguiSystems, Inc.

Handout: 9 Tips for Asking Questions

Many students need to learn how to ask good questions. This handout includes some strategies your students can use to ask effective questions during listening. Tell them that good listeners ask questions to help them understand something better. Asking the speaker to repeat herself or to give more examples is a good way for the listener to clarify the message. Explain to your students that the need to ask questions doesn't mean they're ignorant or not paying attention.

Listening to Ask Questions

Now your students are ready to practice their new questioning skills. Ask each student to take out a sheet of paper. As your students listen to some messages you'll read, have them write questions that will help them understand each message. Ask your students to share their questions with each other. This activity will show your students that different people may have different questions about the same message.

On the other hand, individual students will see that other students may have the same questions they do. Your students will learn the value of asking appropriate questions to improve listening comprehension. You'll find the messages to read and questions your students might ask on pages 120 and 121.

Additional Activities

★ Have your students observe other listeners' behaviors during a class, an assembly, or a staff meeting at work. Have your students list the verbal and nonverbal feedback behaviors they hear and see. Which behaviors contributed to effective listening? Which behaviors got in the way of effective listening?

★ Write the following verbal and nonverbal behaviors on index cards.

1. verbal – wait too long to respond
2. verbal – judge the speaker: "I think that's stupid." "You're wrong for doing that."
3. verbal – ask too many questions
4. verbal – ask an unrelated question or interrupt
5. verbal – do not answer a question, just keep talking
6. nonverbal – poor eye contact, look away
7. nonverbal – stand too close or keep backing away
8. nonverbal – give inappropriate facial expressions
9. nonverbal – poor posture: slump over, turn away from your partner
10. nonverbal – yawn

Next, let each student choose a partner. Have each pair choose a card, then have a conversation on any topic in front of the class. Encourage one member of the pair to exhibit the inappropriate behavior that's written on the card he chose. Have the rest of the class identify the inappropriate feedback behavior. Finally, have each pair role-play again, this time using appropriate verbal or nonverbal feedback.

★ Have each student keep a log of the type of questions he asks during a typical day. Then, discuss the questions different students ask. Do students tend to ask questions that clarify, questions that ask the speaker to repeat, or questions that encourage further discussion of the topic? Let your students determine what kind of listeners they might be, based on the questions they ask.

★ Give your students the opportunity to apply question-asking strategies. During your lessons, exhibit behaviors or provide information you feel would lead your students to ask questions. You might be vague, use unknown words, talk too fast, give too much information at once, leave out a step in your directions, or start a thought but not finish it. Reinforce any questions that are asked, noting whether the question was specific. For example, you might say, "I'm glad you asked me what that word means. Now I know exactly how to help you understand."

5 Ways to Give Verbal Feedback

It might sound strange, but good listeners don't always just listen. Good listeners also respond to the speaker and to his message. When you respond with words to a message, you're giving *verbal feedback*.

Verbal feedback lets the speaker know if you agree with her message. It also lets the speaker know if you're confused by her message. Most importantly, verbal feedback lets the speaker know if you're interested in what she's saying.

The speaker depends on you to let her know if you understand her message. Your verbal feedback helps you and the speaker communicate better.

98 Decide when you should give verbal feedback.

Sometimes you can give feedback at any time during the message. But at other times, you should wait until the speaker has finished talking.

For example, during a casual classroom discussion, it's usually okay to give feedback at any time. Your teachers often encourage you to speak up whenever you have a question or a comment. Just be sure you don't interrupt anyone.

When you're at the movie theater or listening to a guest speaker, though, it's usually better to wait to give feedback. Some speakers might ask you to hold your questions until they're finished speaking. If you need to wait, write your questions down so you don't forget them.

99 Practice giving verbal feedback.

You probably give verbal feedback more often than you think. The simplest form of verbal feedback encourages someone to keep talking. When you say, "Uh-huh. Yeah go on. I hear you." or "What happened then?" you're giving excellent verbal feedback. You're showing the speaker that you're interested in her message.

Verbal feedback is easy to give after you practice it a few times.

5 Ways to Give Verbal Feedback, *continued*

100 Don't judge the speaker.

Try to respond to the speaker's message, not to the speaker's personality. You might disagree with someone's opinion, and that's okay. But be sure the speaker doesn't feel that you're putting him down.

101 Show you're interested in the speaker's topic.

Tell the speaker you thought his topic was very interesting. You can encourage him to tell you more by asking, "Could you tell me more about . . . ?" Or you could tell him his message reminded you of something and share what you know about the topic.

102 When the speaker is finished, share any information you have.

You might know something about the speaker's topic. Feel free to share what you know with the speaker. Many good conversations begin when people share information about a subject they're both interested in.

5 Ways to Improve Your Verbal Feedback

Has a friend ever told you he didn't like something you said several days after you said it? You probably would have liked to have heard your friend's feelings sooner.

The same is true of many speakers. Most speakers want your verbal feedback *as soon as possible*. Verbal feedback is very helpful to the speaker. Helpful feedback improves communication between you and the speaker.

The five tips below will help you give verbal feedback that's very helpful to the speaker.

103 Give specific feedback.

It's very helpful to the speaker if you tell him exactly how you feel about his message. For example, suppose your best friend embarrasses you in front of your other friends. You might want to say, "What's your problem? Don't be such a jerk!"

But a response like that doesn't tell your friend how you feel. Instead you might say, "Look, it makes me feel bad when you talk that way about me." Then your friend will know exactly how you feel. She'll be able to change her behavior if she wants to.

104 When possible, give immediate feedback.

Your feedback will be more helpful if you give it soon after hearing a message. If you think someone has given a super speech, he'll appreciate hearing your opinion right away. If you think you deserved a *B* rather than *C* on a project, talk to your teacher soon after you receive your grade. Remember, you want information to be clear to both you and the speaker. So give your response while everything is still fresh in your mind.

105 Give the speaker feedback when he asks for it.

You've probably been in many situations when a speaker has asked, "Are there any questions?" or "Is there anything you don't understand?" and no one said anything. When no one responds to these kinds of questions, the speaker can't tell if his message is clear.

If you understand the speaker's message, say so! If you have questions, ask them. The speaker needs to know if his message got through to you.

5 Ways to Improve Your Verbal Feedback, *continued*

106 Thank the speaker for his time and information.

Most people have very busy schedules. It's good communication to thank someone for sharing information. Even the simplest verbal exchanges can be improved this way. If your friend tells you he'll pick you up for the wrestling match, tell him that you appreciate his gesture.

107 Realize that your feedback might not be rewarded.

Most speakers appreciate your helpful feedback. But just because you offer feedback doesn't mean the speaker will respond to you in words. Don't get discouraged, though. He might choose a different way to show he appreciates your feedback. He might nod or smile to show he's glad you liked what he has to say.

9 Ways to Give Nonverbal Feedback

Think of a time you've rolled your eyes at something someone has said. What did it mean when you rolled your eyes? When you respond to a message without using words, you're using *nonverbal feedback*.

A speaker needs your nonverbal feedback to know if her message is getting across to you.

She also uses your nonverbal feedback to see how you feel about what she's saying.

Nonverbal feedback can be more powerful than verbal feedback. Many speakers pay more attention to what they *see* in their audiences than to what they *hear* from their audiences.

The following tips will help you give nonverbal feedback.

108 Face the speaker.

Looking at the speaker shows you're ready to listen to her. If you're turned away from the speaker, she has to guess whether or not you're listening. She might think you're daydreaming or uninterested in her message. By facing the speaker, you can show you're interested while you pay attention.

109 Make eye contact.

Making eye contact means looking at someone's eyes. If you asked a store clerk a question and he didn't look up at you, what would you think? You might think he didn't want to help you.

Making eye contact means you're interested in what someone is saying. Keeping eye contact can help you concentrate better on what the speaker is saying.

110 Sit up straight.

Your body posture lets the speaker know if you're interested or not. Good posture shows you're alert and paying attention. Bad posture makes you look like you don't care about what the speaker is saying.

If you slumped in your chair, the speaker might think you're bored or confused. But if you lean slightly forward, the speaker will think you're interested in his message. Sitting up straight will help you pay attention, too.

111 Take notes.

If you're listening to a lecture, write down the points that confuse you or that you disagree with. Your notes will help you remember questions you want to ask. Plus, the speaker will see that you're interested enough in his message to take notes.

9 Ways to Give Nonverbal Feedback, *continued*

112 Use facial expressions.

Facial expressions show how we feel about
what we hear and see. What would you think
if you saw your friend frowning at his report
card? By the look on his face, you might think
your friend was unhappy with his grades.

Using facial expressions gives the speaker
nonverbal feedback. When you're listening to
a speaker, the look on your face will tell him if
you're confused or if something he says suddenly
becomes clear to you.

You might raise your eyebrows if you're surprised.
Or, you might frown a little to show you're confused
and you want the speaker to explain something.
One of the best ways to give positive feedback to
anyone is to smile!

113 Give nonverbal feedback often.

Speakers need to know that you're following their messages. If you give plenty of
feedback, the speaker will know if you understand what he's saying. It's up to you to
do everything you can to understand a message.

By seeing your nonverbal feedback, the speaker will be able to communicate with you
better. And better communication is the reward for good listening!

114 Give nonverbal feedback at any time during the speaker's message.

Your *5 Ways to Give Verbal Feedback* handout says that you should sometimes wait until
the end of a message to respond verbally. But that doesn't mean you can't respond at
all. You can give nonverbal feedback at any time during a message. You can smile, nod,
look confused, or take notes.

Remember, you can let the speaker know how you feel without saying a word!

9 Ways to Give Nonverbal Feedback, *continued*

115 Watch for nonverbal feedback that sends a negative message.

So far, you've learned how to send positive nonverbal feedback. But some kinds of feedback are negative. Anything that distracts someone's attention away from the speaker is negative nonverbal feedback.

Looking out the window, tapping your pencil, yawning, passing notes, and rolling your eyes are examples of negative nonverbal feedback. This type of feedback tells the speaker that you're bored and not interested.

Remember, negative nonverbal feedback is very frustrating to the speaker. There are positive ways to let someone know you're confused or bored without being rude. You could ask a question or apologize if you're having trouble paying attention to the speaker.

116 Be careful not to send "mixed messages."

Try to make your nonverbal feedback agree with your verbal feedback. Otherwise, you could send a mixed message to someone. Your mixed message might be confusing.

For example, when you meet someone for the first time, your message will be very clear if you smile and say, "I'm very glad to meet you."

But if you yawn and look away when you say, "I'm very glad to meet you," the person will know you're not glad to meet him at all. You need to decide which message you really want to send.

Give Me Some Feedback!

Name _____

Your emotions often determine the feedback you give in a certain situation. Read the emotions below and think about times you've felt each one. Then, write the kinds of verbal and nonverbal feedback you might give to show your feelings. The first one is done for you as an example.

Emotion	Verbal	Nonverbal
1. happy	*"I feel great today!"*	*smile, give thumbs-up sign*
2. angry		
3. bored		
4. excited		
5. embarrassed		
6. worried		
7. proud		
8. confused		

Mixed Messages

When you give verbal and nonverbal feedback, it's easy to send mixed messages. In each situation below, circle the verbal feedback and underline the nonverbal feedback.

Then, tell why the two types of feedback don't go together well. Finally, tell how the speaker could have given more effective, more truthful feedback.

1. Joy and Linda met at the library on Saturday to study for a test. Linda looked pale and she was coughing. Joy asked Linda if she felt like studying today.

   "Yeah," said Linda, "I'm fine!"

2. "Are you still mad at me, Melody?" asked Donna.

   Melody folded her arms, rolled her eyes, and turned away from Donna.

   "No," Melody said, "don't worry about it."

3. Mr. Christensen walked up to Phillip and a friend in the hallway. "Phillip! I'm glad I caught you!" he said. "The Science Fair Committee meeting has been cancelled."

   Phillip grinned and winked at his friend.

   "Oh, that's too bad, Mr. Christensen," replied Phillip. "I really wanted to go."

4. Alberto was telling Daniel about his visit to Spain. Daniel took a deep sigh and looked at the clock on the dresser. Then he leaned back in his chair and yawned. "Are you listening to me?" asked Alberto.

   "Yeah! So go ahead, how was the food over there?" replied Daniel.

Mixed Messages

5. Mark's little sister, Monica, leaped from behind his bedroom door and yelled, "Boo!" Mark's eyes widened and he jumped backwards.

   "You didn't scare me, Monica. I knew you were there all along," Mark said.

6. Max was sitting at his computer on the first day of his new job. He felt dumb because he didn't know how to put the disk in. He started to sweat. His supervisor came by and asked, "So, can you figure that machine out?"

   "Sure," said Max. "No problem."

7. Audrey and Claire were whispering about something that happened after last Friday's basketball game. Jim walked by and leaned in to hear what the girls were saying. Claire snapped, "I suppose you want to hear about it, too, Jim."

   "No," said Jim, "I really don't care."

8. Greg saw Paul talking to Kim. Paul and Kim were smiling, laughing, and leaning toward each other as they talked. After Kim went to class, Greg went up to Paul and asked, "Hey, you and Kim are getting along pretty well, huh? Do you like her?"

   Paul quickly replied, "No way! She's kind of weird!"

9. Jason caught up with Pang in the hallway. "You promised you'd call me about skateboarding on Saturday. What happened?" Jason asked.

   Pang looked at the floor.

   "I was going to," he said, "but my parents decided to have this family get-together and I just ran out of time."

9 Tips for Asking Questions

What's the best way to be sure you understand something? Ask questions about it! Good listeners ask questions when they don't understand things or when something interferes with their listening.

Your responsibility as a listener is to make sure you understand the speaker's message. By asking questions, you improve your chances of really understanding what you're listening to.

The nine tips in this handout will help you ask good questions.

117 Wait until the speaker has finished before you ask questions.

You might be eager to ask a question. But if you wait for the speaker to finish, she might answer your question on her own.

118 Write questions down as you think of them.

Since you're going to wait until the speaker is finished, you should write down any questions you have. That way, you'll remember what you want to ask.

If you don't have time to write the whole question, write a few key words that will help you remember.

119 Ask specific questions.

Don't just ask "Huh?" or "What's that mean?" Ask clear questions so the speaker knows exactly how to help you.

120 Try to ask questions that are related to the topic.

Try to avoid asking questions that have nothing to do with the topic. If you want to discuss another topic, wait until the speaker is completely finished with his presentation.

121 Ask the speaker to define words you don't know.

If the speaker uses a word you've never heard before, say, "What does *replenish* mean?" or "I'm not sure what *oxidize* means."

9 Tips for Asking Questions, *continued*

122 Tell the speaker if you missed part of her message.

Everyone gets distracted now and then. People or noises might distract you. Sometimes you simply can't hear everything the speaker is saying. Other times, the speaker might have spoken too quickly.

The easiest solution is to ask the speaker to repeat himself. Say, "I'm sorry, I didn't catch what you said. Would you mind repeating it?" Then, thank the speaker for taking time to help you.

123 If you're not sure what a message means, ask the speaker to explain it again.

Not every message is easy to understand. If you're confused, ask the speaker to explain his message. Say, "I'm confused about the last thing you said. Can you explain it again?"

124 Remember, any question that helps you understand is a good question.

Asking questions shows you're interested in the speaker's message. Asking questions lets the speaker know that you want to learn. Asking questions doesn't mean you're stupid. Asking questions means you're a smart listener!

125 Restate what you think the speaker said.

A good way to check if you've understood a message is to repeat the message to the speaker. Say, "Let me see if I understand what you're saying. Are you saying that . . . ?"

If you have understood correctly, the speaker will tell you. If you've misunderstood the message, the speaker will have a chance to explain his message in a different way.

Listening to Ask Questions

Listen to each message I read. Then, write some questions that help you understand the message better.

You might want to ask me to repeat a part of the message, to define a word, or to explain something so it's clearer to you.

1. Let's go see this movie. It starts at 7:15.

    What's the name of the movie?
    Where is the movie playing?

2. (Create an auditory distraction during the underlined part of the message. You might scoot your chair, shuffle some papers, drop or close a book, or cough.)

    Before you leave today, be sure to fill out parts <u>A and B</u> and the personal information section on your permission forms.

    Which parts should I fill out?
    What am I supposed to fill out?

3. As you leave the auditorium, pick one or the other and return it soon.

    What should I pick?
    When exactly should I return it?

4. Now that you've chosen topics for your persuasive speeches, I'd like you to locate three sources at the Resource Center that substantiate your argument.

    What's a persuasive speech?
    How many sources should I look for?
    What does substantiate *mean?*

5. (Read quickly.) It's time to register for next year's classes. Line up in alphabetical order. If your last name begins with *A* through *L,* go to the south gym. If your last name begins with *M* through *Z,* proceed to the north foyer.

    I couldn't understand the directions. Could you repeat them more slowly?
    Where is the north foyer?
    Where should I go?

6. Take the 10th Street bus to the subway entrance. Get off there and ride until you get to 80th Avenue North. I'll meet you at the corner.

    Where do I get off the bus?
    What subway do I ride to 80th Avenue North?
    At which corner will you meet me?

7. Please ask the following students to report to the Guidance Office at 2:00: Van, Tim, Veronica, Josh, Mandy, Tina, Kirk, Anthony, and Rachel.

    Could you repeat those names more slowly?
    Could you give me those names two at a time?
    Where should the students go?
    When should the students be at the guidance office?

8. Because everyone brought a plethora of food and beverages to the reunion last year, please sign up to bring only one.

    What does plethora mean?
    Should I bring food or a beverage?

9. The semicolon is used between independent clauses which are not connected by coordinating conjunctions.

    What's a semicolon/independent clause/coordinating conjunction?
    Could you give me an example?

10. For the following exercise, I'd like you to read each of the paragraphs, delete extraneous material, underline all the topic sentences, and place a check next to the paragraphs that are acceptable.

    What does delete/extraneous mean?
    Could you review topic sentences?
    What's an acceptable paragraph?
    Could you say the directions one at a time?

11. (Create an auditory distraction, such as coughing, clearing your throat, scooting your chair, or shuffling papers during the underlined part of the message.)

    Attention Spanish Club members. Today's meeting will begin at <u>3:45</u> rather than 3:30. Thank you.

    I didn't catch the new meeting time. Could you repeat it?

12. (Read quickly.) We need a loaf of bread, a dozen eggs, milk, a head of lettuce, three rolls of paper towels, iced tea mix, 2 cans of green beans, and a case of whatever kind of soda pop you like.

    Will you say the list again?
    How much milk should I get?
    Could you speak more slowly, please?

References

Hunsaker, Richard A. *Understanding and Developing the Skills of Oral Communication: Speaking and Listening*. Englewood, CO: Morton Publishing Company, 1982.

Marzanno, Robert J. and Daisy E. Arredondo. *Tactics for Thinking*. Aurora, CO: Mid-continent Regional Education Laboratory, 1986.

Robinson, Suzanne and Deborah Deutsch Smith. "Listening Skills: Teaching Learning Disabled Students to be Better Listeners." *Focus on Exceptional Children 3*, no. 9 (April 1981).

Wiig, Elisabeth Hemmersam and Eleanor Messing Semel. "Remembering Spoken Messages: Intervention." *Language Assessment and Intervention for the Learning Disabled*. Columbus, OH: Charles E. Merrill Publishing Co., 1980.

Wolvin, Andrew and Carolyn Gwynn Coakley. *Listening*. 3rd Edition. Dubuque, IA: William C. Brown Publishers, 1988.